How to Be Good at Life

A Treasure Chest of Golden Nuggets for a Happier and
More Productive Life That They Don't Teach in School

Andrew G. Robbins

authorHOUSE®

AuthorHouse™
1663 Liberty Drive
Bloomington, IN 47403
www.authorhouse.com
Phone: 1 (800) 839-8640

Published by AuthorHouse 11/29/2017

ISBN: 978-1-5462-1703-9 (sc)
ISBN: 978-1-5462-1702-2 (e)

Print information available on the last page.

Any people depicted in stock imagery provided by Thinkstock are models,
and such images are being used for illustrative purposes only.
Certain stock imagery © Thinkstock.

This book is printed on acid-free paper.

Because of the dynamic nature of the Internet, any web addresses or links contained
in this book may have changed since publication and may no longer be valid. The views
expressed in this work are solely those of the author and do not necessarily reflect the
views of the publisher, and the publisher hereby disclaims any responsibility for them.

English Standard Version (ESV)
The Holy Bible, English Standard Version. ESV® Text Edition: 2016. Copyright ©
2001 by Crossway Bibles, a publishing ministry of Good News Publishers.

New International Version (NIV)
Holy Bible, New International Version®, NIV® Copyright ©1973, 1978, 1984, 2011
by Biblica, Inc.® Used by permission. All rights reserved worldwide.

New Living Translation (NLT)
Holy Bible, New Living Translation, copyright © 1996, 2004, 2007, 2013,
2015 by Tyndale House Foundation. Used by permission of Tyndale House
Publishers Inc., Carol Stream, Illinois 60188. All rights reserved.

King James Version (KJV)
Scriptures are taken from the King James Version of the Bible - Public Domain.

New American Standard Bible (NASB)
Copyright © 1960, 1962, 1963, 1968, 1971, 1972, 1973, 1975, 1977, 1995
by The Lockman Foundation

For my children, children-in-law, and grandchildren:

Hannah, Noah, and Evangeline
Luke and Hope
Drew
and all who will come after you in your family lines.

May your own lives be blessed with the second greatest gift that God gives – second only to salvation itself: the Gift of Wisdom.

"Listen to your father, who gave you life, and do not despise your mother when she is old. Get the truth and never sell it; also get wisdom, discipline, and good judgment. The father of godly children has cause for joy. What a pleasure to have children who are wise. So give your father and mother joy! May she who gave you birth be happy. O, my son, give me your heart. May your eyes take delight in following my ways."
-Proverbs 23:22-26

Introduction

"I'm so good at life!"

It's a silly expression that my son, Luke, sometimes playfully uses to congratulate himself on something he has said or done that greatly pleases him. It always makes me laugh when I hear him say it.

Lately I have been thinking more about that phrase and what it means. *Good at life.* There are a lot of people who are good at a lot of things: good at math, good at singing, good at sports, good at business, and good at making people laugh. I know lots of people who are good at many things but who are nevertheless not good at life. Some of the most talented and successful people I know are also some of the unhappiest and most dysfunctional.

How, then, does a person become good at life? What does that even mean?

Before I propose my answer, I feel I should offer a qualification.

My Disclaimer

In offering this guidebook on how to be good at life, I am, of course, appearing to present myself as some sort of expert on the subject. I will hasten to add, therefore, that I am nothing of the sort. After more than 50 years of life, I am still on a process of discovery, and I intend to be for the rest of my life. A friend and mentor, Dr. Jerry King, one of the most learned men I know, said to me at the age of 78 that he is on the steepest learning curve of his life. That's how I feel right now as I write this book.

Even so, I have learned a thing or two in 50 years. I have grown and developed and become successful in some respects, I suppose. And while I understand that I don't know all that I will someday, I have also learned one important principle in life is to "pay it forward." In other words, when life blesses you with some sort of gift from heaven, whether it be a free meal or the treasure of a nugget of wisdom, take that with which you have been blessed and pass it on. That's what I'm doing here.

I have made many mistakes in my life, and I have a lot of regrets. I have learned from many of those mistakes, however, and I hope that what I have learned will help someone else, particularly my children and grandchildren. It is my goal with this book to become your own personal landmine sweeper. In the military there are people who are trained to identify and eliminate landmines so that others can march on without being severely injured or killed. In many respects I have already walked the landmine field and been blown up numerous times myself. If I can show you, the reader, how to avoid these same landmines, then I have accomplished my mission.

I wish to also add that there are many more principles pertaining to being good at life that cannot be covered in one book. Going out and finding those nuggets for yourself is a principle in and of itself: *seek out wisdom and be a constant learner.* This, too, is part of what it means to be good at life.

So let's get back to the question as to what being good at life means and how to achieve it.

I have distilled the answer to those questions into my own simple definition:

Being good at life means making a positive impact on the world that endures long after you are gone from this life, and being happy and fulfilled while helping others to feel happy and fulfilled. It means growing, learning, and developing as a course of habit, and it means knowing God and finding delight in walking with your Savior.

The back end of that definition is not something I will be able to expound upon in this book. Knowing God and finding delight in walking with your Savior might take another entire book to unravel. But on the other hand, it might not be that complicated. After all, Jesus taught that in order to find true life you must lay yours down, turn from your selfish ways, and take up your cross and follow Him (see Matthew 16:24). Jesus' entire earthly ministry was devoted to giving of Himself and meeting the spiritual and physical needs of as many people as He could. He asks you and I to do the same.

That same priority is what this book will focus on: following the teachings of Jesus by learning to overcome self-centeredness and living your life as a shining example of God's love toward other people. In doing so, each chapter will offer insights on important life principles – 31 in all – one for each day of the month, plus a bonus section at the end. These principles are those that I feel are vital to master in learning how to be good at life, particularly those having to do with interaction with others. These are the principles I have learned and am still learning – some the hard way. I have tried to live by them and they have helped me in every facet of my life: career, ministry, and relationships in general. They will do the same for you.

Before we begin our 31-day journey, or whatever length of time it takes you to read this book, I will preface the following chapters by reminding you of a principle of education, that "repetition is the mother of learning." I have made a good share of the following chapters short on purpose so that you can go back and easily reread and review. I encourage that, because 31 principles are too many to master in one reading. I recommend two or three readings, at least, in order to keep each principle fresh in your mind and eventually making them part of your daily practice. In fact, I am finding great benefit myself in reviewing these principles and writing them down for you. I have noticed that there are certain practices in this book that I needed a refresher on, even though I have been trying to live by these principles for the last 20 years. Repetition is vital for mastering any skill or principle, just the same as if you were learning to play an instrument or improving your foul shots in basketball.

I also encourage you to carefully read the quotes and scripture passages I have offered at the end of each chapter. They, too, will provide inspiration and additional insight on each subject.

One final note before we begin. It is my aim with this book to help you to someday feel a twinge of embarrassment about the person you are right now, as well as a sense of satisfaction. That might seem contradictory, but everyone who grows as a matter of habit experiences both. As we develop in knowledge, good judgment, and life experience, we look back over the landscape of our lives through the lenses of the wisdom gained over the years and roll our eyes at how foolish we were at times. Nearly everyone experiences this to a degree, but some more than others. The ones who have applied themselves to being students of life may feel the greatest degree of embarrassment at the poor judgments of their youth simply because they eventually learn to identify rashness, recklessness or inconsiderate behavior more than others. However, it is also these who enjoy the enduring profits of the wisdom they have gained and the good choices that have accumulated as the years roll by.

If you are a young adult, on the other hand, and you begin applying yourself to gaining wisdom while in your youth, you will avoid many of the landmines of life that cause the agonizing regret plaguing much of humanity, and you will feel much less embarrassment in comparison as you contemplate your short time on this planet. That's where the satisfaction comes in. If you are a young person reading this book, my prayer is that the principles you are about to read will one day cause you to look back over your life feeling a little silly about youthful imprudence, but also help you to experience that thankful sense of satisfaction that you did, even in your youth, often practice the discretion that leads to a wonderful life.

Let's begin now learning how to be good – or at least a little better, perhaps – at life.

> *"Feed your mind. Sharpen your interest in two major subjects: life and people. Learn how you can better interact with others."*
> *-Jim Rohn*

1

The Attitude than Changes Your Altitude

On a summer day many years ago I was gazing through the windshield of my car at nothing in particular as I sat at a stoplight, obsessing over something in my life that I wanted desperately to be different. That day I had sunk into a mild depression as I mulled over my situation, not knowing what awaited me at that intersection. As I waited for the light to turn green, suddenly my darkened countenance was interrupted by a certain pedestrian crossing the road in front of me. The man caught my attention because he was very different than the others who hastily passed by at the pace of a busy life. Walking slowly and deliberately, this man wore dark sunglasses and tapped the ground in front of him with a walking stick. Then, as if an invisible force took me by the chin and redirected my focus the way a parent does when trying to help a little one see something really special out the window of a car before it passes by, I almost reflexively turned and looked off to my right where I noticed a school for the blind.

I sat there briefly frozen, taking in the personal revelation of what I was seeing. The blind man and the school he had apparently just come from may have gone unnoticed to dozens of other people who were at the scene that day, but for me it was a life-defining encounter; a moment burned in my memory, because it was as if God had come to me and painted me a picture like only He can, vivid and full of meaning. And just as suddenly as that blind man burst on the scene, my countenance immediately lifted as I watched him slowly make his way out of sight. As bad as I thought I had it at the time, I realized how blessed I was to have the gift of sight – a gift that is worth a billion dollars! As my focus was redirected on what was good and right with my life rather than the small things that had seized upon my thoughts, despondency was replaced with thankfulness.

Thankfulness does not come naturally to fallen mankind. Because of the perverting influence of sin, we tend to think mostly in terms of what we do not have rather than what we do have. We may be situated in comfortable, temperature-controlled housing with many amenities, eat three hearty meals per day, and drive a late-model car. Yet in spite of these blessings we tend to focus on what few things may be wrong in our lives and so obsess over them that they rob us of the enjoyment in life we should be experiencing.

Success gurus teach that you attract more of whatever you think about most of the time. This concept is consistent with Proverbs 23:7, which says in the King James Version that "as a man thinketh in his heart, so is he." While the description is too lengthy to explain in this format, the concept of "attraction" is validated by discoveries in quantum physics. The predominant beliefs and thoughts of a person appear to attract more of those same things.

A study was once conducted to attempt to prove or disprove that what people believe about themselves is a predictor of what their futures hold. Researchers selected two groups of people: those who believed that life is good and they are generally lucky people, and those who believed that they are unlucky and that life never seems to give them a break. After analyzing the events that occurred in the lives of these two groups of people over a long period of time, the researchers concluded that what one believes about himself is indeed an accurate predictor of the kind of life a person leads. Good things seemed to consistently happen to those in the study who were thankful for their lives and believed that they were just lucky people, while unfortunate things seemed to happen fairly frequently to those in the opposite group whose outlook on life was negative, who believed they were just unlucky and who did not practice lifestyles of thankfulness.

For probably 99% of Americans, it's not too difficult to find something for which to be thankful. When you consider the fact that most of the rest of the world lives in abject poverty compared to most Americans, and if you know some of the details about how people in other countries live, it gives you a completely different perspective on your own life.

This is what visiting Haiti in 1984 did for me. The poverty I saw there was so shocking that the images of the people I saw there are still riveted in my mind all these many years later. I was raised poor by American standards, but the suffering I witnessed in Haiti made me feel like I was rich!

Only a year or so after my Haiti trip I visited the man, Robbie King, who became my step-brother when my mother married his father. Robbie had developed multiple sclerosis, a terrible disease that I knew nothing about until I saw his shriveled and contorted body lying in a bed at the facility where he stayed. The disease had robbed him of all muscle control. He could not speak. He could barely move. His limbs were drawn in and twisted. The only way he could communicate was to use what little muscle control he had in his fingers to point to images on a chart that helped his care-givers know what he needed. All he could do all day was stare at a constantly-running television in his room. And that's how he lived out the rest of his life.

My mother was a natural caregiver and would take it upon herself to stretch out Robbie's arms and legs when she visited him, which was a necessary but painful therapy. On the day we visited Robbie together, she attempted to gently straighten out his drawn up legs, and as she did I watched as a grimace of pain contorted Robbie's face. His plight was already so pitiful that watching him writhe in agony was like a knife going through my soul. On the way home I sat in the back seat of the car and quietly wept. It was a difficult thing for me to see, but it gave me a glimpse of how much suffering there really is in the world, and how spared I have been from most of it.

My message here on this point of thankfulness is two-fold:

First, live your life in a constant attitude of gratitude for those things that have been mercifully and graciously given by God's benevolent hand. Your situation in life could always be worse, and you have indeed been blessed with so much. Live your life in thankfulness to God, and resist the temptation to grumble, complain, and focus only on your problems, or compare yourself to those who seem to have it better than you. Remember, you will get more of what you tend to think about most of the time.

Secondly, be lavish in how you express thankfulness to the people in your life who have blessed you in various ways. Don't ever assume that people know how much you love them. Tell them! Don't ever assume that people know how much you appreciate them. Tell them! And don't ever assume that people know you are thankful for something nice they have done for you. Demonstrate that thankfulness by telling them, and not only telling them, but being so thankful that those same people are delighted that they helped you or gave to you in some way. Be in the habit of sending people cards or nice messages. Facebook is a very good way to express your thankfulness for certain people, because you can thank them and praise them publicly and make them feel really good about themselves …and feel really good about *you*! Those kinds of gestures are never wasted. If you are not in the habit of being expressively thankful, however, don't be surprised when people don't want to give to you or help you anymore.

I like to say that the attitude of gratitude will change your altitude. Just as an airplane's altitude will change according to a "nose up" or "nose down" attitude, people's predominant attitudes will similarly determine how high in life they go.

Thankfulness is a "nose up" attitude. The more thankful you are, the higher in life you will tend to go.

To demonstrate how certain matters that are truly not very important in the grand scheme of things can get us down if our focus isn't in the right place, I honestly don't even remember what it was that made me so depressed that day those many years ago when God arrested my attention at that stoplight. I vividly remember that blind man, however, and the lesson he taught me.

"Rejoice always, pray continually, give thanks in all circumstances; for this is God's will for you in Christ Jesus."
-1 Thessalonians 5:16-18 (NIV)

"Do not be anxious about anything, but in every situation, by prayer and petition, with thanksgiving, present your requests to God. And the peace of God, which transcends all understanding, will guard your hearts and your minds in Christ Jesus. Finally, brothers and sisters, whatever is true, whatever is noble, whatever is right, whatever is pure, whatever is lovely, whatever is admirable--if anything is excellent or praiseworthy--think about such things."
-Philippians 4:6-8 (NIV)

"Do not indulge in dreams of having what you have not, but reckon up the chief of the blessings you do possess, and then thankfully remember how you would crave for them if they were not yours."
- Marcus Aurelius

"We would worry less if we praised more. Thanksgiving is the enemy of discontent and dissatisfaction."
 - **H.A. Ironside**

2

Basin Theology

Bruce Thielemann, pastor of the First Presbyterian Church in Pittsburgh, once told of a conversation he had with a man who challenged his paradigm on serving. "You preachers talk a lot about giving," the man said, "but when you get right down to it, it all comes down to basin theology."

"Basin theology? What's that," Pastor Thielemann asked.

The man explained, "Remember what Pilate did when he had the chance to acquit Jesus? He called for a basin and washed his hands of the whole thing. But Jesus, the night before His death, called for a basin and proceeded to wash the feet of the disciples. It all comes down to basin theology. Which basin will you choose?"

In other words, the man was suggesting that giving and serving must be more than simply lip service. It has to be lived out to be worth anything.

The truly successful person – that is, successful at life, successful at being happy and fulfilled, not necessarily successful in the eyes of the world – is the person who understands that his/her purpose in life is to take that which God has given – talents, money, resources, etc. – and use them to serve mankind in some way, large or small; to make someone else's load lighter, to help lift someone up to a better place, to help other people feel significant, and to play a role in expanding God's Kingdom on the earth in whatever way you can.

There have been many people over whose talent and knowledge I have marveled. Yet in many cases, the abilities of those who possess extraordinary talent are not really serving mankind in any significant way.

As I write this, I'm thinking of a man who is a very talented musician. We attended the same church for a while and I was always curious why he sat in the pews Sunday after Sunday and was not participating in the worship ministry since they could definitely have used his help. I asked him one day why he wasn't playing on the worship team, and he said something to the effect that it was too much work. It was true that he had experienced some relational difficulties in the past in serving on a previous worship team, which, incidentally, he had himself instigated. So he let his next church's worship team struggle while he did nothing. Today, he is not in church at all the last I heard, but is the guitarist in a cover band playing secular rock music. I wonder if that's what God had in mind when He blessed this man with musical talent: playing rock music in whatever venue he and his buddies can find while nearby churches struggle in piecing together enough musicians to make the Sunday morning worship experience pleasing and meaningful.

There is one common theme woven throughout this book, and that's this:

IT'S NOT ABOUT YOU!

I read a sign once that said, *"There is no one so empty as the person who is full of self."* A person whose life consists of little more than glorying in his own accomplishments and seeking out his own pleasure and who doesn't understand that he was placed upon this earth to serve a purpose bigger than himself is misguided indeed. A person who sees other people as a means to an end rather than the very reason for one's existence – to serve them – is bankrupt in his soul. But the person who knows how to serve, how to be a blessing, how to give generously of their money, talents and time, and how to take instruction graciously is a person who is on God's road to promotion both in this life and the one to come.

You Must Overcome Shyness to Serve Well

My personality tends toward shyness. I learned early in life, however, how paralyzing shyness can be, so I made efforts to overcome it. A revelation that helped me in that process is the understanding that shyness is almost totally self-centered in many cases. This may be a surprising statement to some readers, but think about it. The embarrassment and awkwardness that accompanies shyness is an emphasis on "me," without any thought of how others may be feeling. Shyness is a manifestation of insecurity, and believe it or not, insecurity has its roots in pride. This may seem counterintuitive, because most people see shyness as a form of humility. Well, because I'm not a psychologist and because I don't know the intricacies of every person's psyche, I certainly cannot speak for everyone who struggles with shyness. It is my guess, however, that shyness for many, if not most, is definitely not a manifestation of humility, because most of the time when shyness makes its appearance it gives no consideration to other people and makes no efforts to be a blessing. It only seeks to withdrawal from people or situations that it interprets as uncomfortable. As Andre Dubus perceptively said, *"Shyness has a strange element of narcissism, a [misguided] belief that how we look, how we perform, is truly important to others."*

In order to be others-focused, it is imperative to overcome shyness. You will never realize your potential or serve others the way you otherwise could if you are crippled with bashfulness.

For example, I have been in social situations numerous times where the shyest people in the room are also the most inconsiderate. Because I have struggled in the past with shyness myself, as I said, I am sympathetic with the discomforts associated with this tendency and my heart always goes to out the bashful.

So I always make an effort in social settings to engage people who seem withdrawn and shy so that they are not left out. There have been times when I have greeted or tried to converse with people who are painfully shy, however, where my efforts are met with either no response at all, or if there *is* a response, it is emotionless, expressionless one-word answers that eventually causes me to give up and move on. While my degree of sympathy toward bashful people has never waned, that sympathy will not prevent me from calling this type of social coldness what it is, or at least what it appears on the surface to be. Any aloofness, regardless of the reason, is often interpreted by others as being rude.

To be fair, I do understand that shy people are not trying to be rude on purpose, and I also recognize that there are powerful neurotransmitter imbalances in some people that lead to almost crushing anxiety in certain situations, or social phobias that are so strong it defies explanation. For those, it might be a good idea to explore some medical help. While I am not one to quickly advocate the pharmaceutical approach to solving one's problems, there is merit, in some extreme cases, to taking properly-prescribed anti-anxiety medications, at least occasionally when one might need to take the edge off the anxiety associated with social situations. Nutritional supplements can also be very helpful, especially the amino acid, L-theanine, which has a calming effect.

Speaking of rudeness, it can also be seen as rude and selfish for the gregarious, life-of-the-party kind of people to busy themselves "working the room" just to shine the spotlight on themselves without any consideration to making things more comfortable for the socially awkward people in the room. People who are truly at peace with themselves don't need to position themselves as the center of attention. They can be content being in the shadows so long as they are helping other people to shine and making efforts at easing the discomforts of the "wall flowers."

Something I wish I could say to all socially awkward people is that it's not difficult to at least fake it. I wish I could tell some people that their faces won't break if they at least smile and make an attempt at being pleasant. I have walked away from some interactions with even people who work a front desk at a business or who wait tables complaining to myself about how inconsiderate I was treated. But then as I think back over some of those interactions, I can easily identify signs of shyness or lack of social skills more than an outright attempt at being rude. Regardless of what is in the heart of the shy person, however, it is the *appearance* of one's behavior to other people that is critical. A shy person might consider himself or herself humble and meek or even fearful, but other people may see that same person as unmannerly. For that reason, too, shy people miss out on a lot in life.

So I say again, shy people should at least try to fake it by beginning with no more than a smile and build on that. A smile can go a long way in making other people feel more at ease around you.

When I came to realize how rude and unmannerly I may have appeared to some people with my shyness, I began making strides to overcome that tendency and actually force myself to be the one who initiates conversations with people instead of waiting for people to approach me. Even after making great strides in that regard, however, a Goliath I had still not slain even into my early forties was public speaking. I had a paralyzing fear of public speaking. So when I began to sense that God was calling me into the ministry, I braced myself like a man and enrolled in a local Toastmaster's club, which is a public speaking group that meets once per week where everyone is expected to stand up and give a speech or monologue of some sort. Because I have had episodes of panic attacks speaking in front of even small groups of people, this seemed like a giant too big to take on. But I did it, and as uncomfortable and stressful as it was, it was helpful in preparing me for the ministry.

If I had made my shyness and fear of public speaking all about me and my security, I would have never broken out of my comfort zone to fight those giants. Because my focus eventually shifted from myself to other people, I was able to muster the courage to grab my sling and run out on the battle field to meet the enemy. I would have never stepped into the destiny that God had in mind for me if I allowed insecurity to rule my life.

In order for you to step into your God-given destiny, you will have to realize that life is not all about just you, but it's about you serving others. And in order to do that, you will have to overcome a few personal obstacles, not the least of which is any insecurities and shyness from which you might be suffering.

If you do suffer from insecurity and shyness, it might be helpful to repeat this phrase to yourself on a regular basis to help overcome that tendency: "It's not about me; it's about others." And even if you don't suffer from shyness, that is still a good phrase to repeat to yourself on a regular basis to remind yourself of why you are on this earth: you are here to serve, not *be* served.

A True Servant is Content to Serve in the Shadows

In closing out this chapter, it necessary to mention that a true servant serves without any thought of credit, payment, or honor for his or her service. Whatever or whoever is being served, the true servant of God's Kingdom is content to serve God by serving people, and allows whatever credit he or she will receive for that service to be bestowed by God. If the service has any ulterior motive of recognition, then it is not true service. Jesus said if we give with the motive in mind of impressing people with our gift, then impressing people is all the reward we will ever get (see Matthew 6:1-4). But if we give discreetly and without positioning ourselves to be noticed, then God will reward us. I have found, in fact, that **the road to your God-given destiny is navigated by selfless service**. If you don't know why God has put you on this earth, just begin serving His Kindgom purposes with whatever talents, abilities, or interests He has bestowed upon you, and in time, His ultimate plan for you will unfold without you trying to make it happen.

It all begins with service.

"Each of you should use whatever gift you have received to serve others, as faithful stewards of God's grace in its various forms."
-1 Peter 4:10 (NIV)

"This is how we know what love is: Jesus Christ laid down his life for us. And we ought to lay down our lives for our brothers and sisters."
-1 John 3:16 (NIV)

"I slept and dreamt that life was joy. I awoke and saw that life was service. I acted and behold, service was joy."
- Rabindranath Tagore

"At the end of life we will not be judged by how many diplomas we have received, how much money we have made, how many great things we have done. We will be judged by 'I was hungry, and you gave me something to eat, I was naked and you clothed me. I was homeless, and you took me in.'"
-Mother Teresa

"Shyness is a curious thing because, like quicksand, it can strike people at any time, and also, like quicksand, it usually makes its victims look down."
-Lemony Snicket

"I'm very shy, so I became outgoing to protect my shyness."
-Don Rickles, Comedian

"Shyness is nice, but shyness can stop you from doing all the things in life you'd like to do."
-Steven Morrisey

3

Planks of Wood and Specks of Sawdust

Around the turn of the 20th Century, Sir Percival Lowell, the world's foremost astronomer at the time, was certain that there were canals on Mars. Venerated for his study of the solar system, Lowell had a particular interest in the "Red Planet."

When Lowell learned in 1877 that an Italian astronomer had seen straight lines crisscrossing the Martian surface, he responded by spending the rest of his life peering through his giant telescope, mapping the channels and canals he saw. He was convinced that the lines he saw was proof of intelligent life on Mars, perhaps an older and more advanced race than humans.

Today we know that Lowell's assumptions about what he saw were false. Space probes have orbited Mars and even landed on its surface. After a thorough mapping of the entire planet, no canals or channels have ever been discovered. How is it that the world's most esteemed astronomer at the time could have seen so much that wasn't there?

There are two possibilities to consider. The first is that he was so infatuated with the idea of intelligent life on Mars that he saw only what he wanted to see, a condition not uncommon among humanity. But the second possibility is that what he saw was actually the result of a rare eye condition from which we now know he suffered. The condition, known today as Lowell's Syndrome, named after the famous astronomer, causes such a profound bulging of the veins of the eyes that those who suffer from this condition can actually see their own eyeball veins in the form of streaks and lines. It's possible that what Lowell was seeing was not Martian canals at all, but actually his own veins!

This condition is reminiscent of the words of Jesus when He warned of seeing "the speck of sawdust" in another person's eye while ignoring the plank in your own (see Matthew 7:1-3). We might consider this tendency of quickly judging others without giving much evaluation to one's own condition as the spiritual equivalent of Lowell's Syndrome. Could it be that it is our tendency to think we see glaring faults in others because we don't want to believe anything better? And could it be that the sharp vision we think we have when viewing other people's shortcomings is, in fact, a view of others distorted by our own disease of self-righteousness and pride?

It has been aptly said that when it comes to seeing the faults of others, we tend to have 20/20 vision, but when seeing our own faults, we are practically blind. And this is likely why the Scriptures condemn passing judgment on others.

> *37"Do not judge, and you will not be judged. Do not condemn, and you will not be condemned. Forgive, and you will be forgiven. 38Give, and it will be given to you. A good measure, pressed down, shaken together and running over, will be poured into your lap. For with the measure you use, it will be measured to you."*
> *-Luke 6:37-38* (NIV)

I had a conversation recently that reminded me of the futility of passing judgment on others. I was catching up with an associate who now works as a therapist for drug addicts. She explained that when it comes to responses to chemical substances like drugs and alcohol, there are four types of people. The first type is the person who has no attraction whatsoever to alcohol or drugs in even small amounts and who never touches any of it. The second type is the person who may enjoy a very occasional glass of wine with a meal, but who could take it or leave it. The third type is the person who drinks alcohol on a fairly regular basis and who may actually develop a mild dependency or full-blown addiction over time due to over-indulgence, but who can, with help, overcome that addiction. But the fourth is the type of person who, because of his or her biochemical uniqueness, can take a single drink of alcohol or one dose of a recreational drug and be instantly and profoundly hooked.

Whatever virtuous qualities you possess, understand that those qualities are God's gift to you, not the other way around. If you are a naturally self-disciplined person who doesn't use drugs or abuse alcohol or who doesn't shirk your responsibilities, don't congratulate yourself as if you have done God or mankind a favor. If those virtues are ones you didn't have to work for but come very naturally, then it is evidence of God's hand upon you. You have not given to God, necessarily, with these virtues. He has given to you. There are many others who do not possess these virtues as a natural part of their personalities. They were raised differently than you, exposed to things – maybe terrible things – that you were not exposed to, they have different personality bents compared to you, and they probably have the broken lives to show for it. Thus, God is judging you by different standards than how He might judge someone who wasn't born with the privileges with which you were born. Because He will require more of you, you must be very honest in evaluating yourself, and slow to pass judgment on others.

This is why the Apostle Paul wrote,

> **"Who are you to condemn someone else's servants? Their own master will judge whether**

> *they stand or fall. And with the Lord's help, they*
> *will stand and receive his approval."*
>   *-Romans 14:4* (NLT)

In order to be good at life, we have to develop the qualities of routinely taking inventory of our own lives while being gracious toward others and allowing God to deal with them. As my wife, Donna, often likes to say, "I don't want to pass judgment because I don't want that to come back on me." Donna, of course, is referring to Jesus' command about judging others. Let's look at it again.

> *"³⁷Do not judge, and you will not be judged.*
> *Do not condemn, and you will not be condemned.*
> *Forgive, and you will be forgiven. ³⁸A good measure,*
> *pressed down, shaken together and running over,*
> *will be poured into your lap. For with the measure*
> *you use, it will be measured to you."*
>   *-Luke 6:37* (NIV)

While it is certainly legitimate to observe the behavior of others and evaluate accordingly, there is a fine line between evaluation and judgment. Evaluation observes behavior only, but stops short of judging that behavior because just observing actions does not always give us the reasons behind them.

For example, I once read a story about a man's three small children who were terrorizing people in a restaurant. They were running around making noise, slapping newspapers out of people's hands, and being completely unruly and disruptive, while the father appeared oblivious to the scene. Finally, a waitress addressed the man firmly and said something along the lines of, "Sir, don't you realize your children are disturbing the other customers? Won't you do something about them?"

The man seemed surprised, as if the waitress's words jolted him out of a daze. "Oh, I'm sorry," he said. "We just came from their mother's funeral, and I guess they don't know how to process it."

The waitress did an immediate about-face and quickly changed her tone. "I'm so sorry!" she said. "Is there anything I can do?"

While it's true that some people can behave very inappropriately, we don't always know the reasons behind it. Therefore, while it is appropriate to evaluate behavior, we should leave the judging to God.

"Brothers and sisters, do not slander one another. Anyone who speaks against a brother or sister or judges them speaks against the law and judges it. When you judge the law, you are not keeping it, but sitting in judgment on it. ¹²There is only one Lawgiver and Judge, the one who is able to save and destroy. But you—who are you to judge your neighbor?*

-James 4:11 (NIV)

"Someone who does not know, and then does something wrong, will be punished only lightly. When someone has been given much, much will be required in return; and when someone has been entrusted with much, even more will be required."

-Luke 12:48 (NLT)

"If anyone thinks they are something when they are not, they deceive themselves. Each one should test their own actions."

-Galatians 6:3-4 (NIV)

4

Tarzan, Jane, and Hungry Leaches

In 1994 the *Chicago Tribune* published a story about two Californians, Randy Curlee and Victoria Ingram, who, after becoming engaged, received some bad news. Since childhood Randy had suffered from diabetes, and, at the time of his engagement to Victoria at the age forty-six, the diabetes had so damaged his kidneys that he needed a transplant to save his life.

The couple listened as Randy's doctor reported the grim facts. Every year only four thousand kidneys become available to the thirty-six thousand people who need a transplant, the doctor said. Usually family members provide the best matches for transplants, but none of his family members were compatible.

Then Victoria broke in. "Why don't you test me?" The doctor conducted the compatibility tests on her, and the couple waited anxiously for the results. Then it happened. They finally got the call that the test results were in, and Victoria's immune system was a perfect match with Randy's.

The couple made plans to be married on October 11, 1994, and then have the transplant operations the following day. But at the last minute the operations had to be delayed because a catheter had nicked Victoria's kidney during her testing. So, one month after their wedding in a five-and-a-half-hour surgery at

Sharp Memorial Hospital in San Diego, Victoria donated her left kidney to her husband, Randy. It was believed to be the first organ donation between a husband and wife in the United States.

In a very literal sense, the marriage of Randy and Victoria Curlee depended on Victoria's sacrifice for its survival. But so does every marriage. Marriages survive and thrive on what each spouse can *give* to their beloved more than what they can *get*.

The Proper Attitude Toward Marriage

Most people enter marriage selfish, looking to their spouse to make them fulfilled and happy, only to find out that it doesn't work that way most of the time. Most people enter marriage like two hungry leaches looking to *get* from the other person, and they eventually suck the life out of each other. Very soon into marriage the imperfections of each spouse are magnified, and they will then often set out to change their husbands and wives. Rather than taking on the maddening and ultimately futile task of changing your spouse, however, the focus must once again turn inward with the goal being to find how to make *yourself* a better person, and how to make your spouse like himself/herself more. The wife should make it her aim to help her man feel like he is her Tarzan, king of the jungle. And the husband must make his ambition to help his wife feel like Jane, queen of the jungle. If you do that, marriage will automatically be more fulfilling, and your spouse will more likely behave more loving and gracious to you as well.

There are times to point out a character flaw or an incorrect way of thinking or behaving, but let this be the rare exception. It should also be understood that no one knows you better than your spouse, and while not every criticism may be valid or offered with the kind of gentleness you prefer, it is important to at least carefully consider the validity of suggestions or criticisms from your spouse. Then reflect on how you might use that criticism to become a better person. While I have not always liked some of the things my wife, Donna, has said to me, ultimately her insights have made me a better person because I have listened and applied the help she has offered. Because Donna's nature is to give, serve and bless me, it makes it easier to listen to her whenever she has something constructive to say. If she was constantly needling me, however, with very little positive input otherwise, I might be more prone to tune her out.

Here's a word to the wise about areas to NEVER criticize in your spouse.

To men, NEVER criticize or make jokes about your wife's looks or weight. Women find much of their self-worth in their looks, and if you criticize that even a little, or even make light-hearted jokes about it, things can get icy very quickly. I have seen men who complain about their overweight wives when they are sporting their own beer bellies. Of course, I happen to believe that both men and women ought to take care of themselves and strive to keep themselves healthy and in relatively good form for the sake of their health and also for the sake of one's spouse, but it is never a good idea to complain about your spouse's weight.

To women, NEVER criticize a man's ability to make money or take care of the family financially, unless, of course, he is truly shirking his God-given responsibilities. Most men find their self-worth in their ability to provide for the family, and if times have become lean, there is no one harder on your husband than himself. A responsible man – one who doesn't gamble or drink away his income – is a man who can easily sink into a depression when money is tight. The thing he needs most during these times is the unconditional support of his wife, not her criticism.

To both husbands and wives, NEVER criticize your spouse's ability to please you in the bedroom. Both sexes find much of their self-worth in their ability to please their spouses sexually. If you make your husband or wife feel insecure in this area, don't be surprised if your love life in and out of the bedroom suffers. If one or both of you is having trouble in knowing just what to do to please the other person, some playful and encouraging guidance might be in order. But never criticize or make jokes.

I was once dining with a group of people that included a couple who had experienced some trouble in their marriage. As we conversed, the wife of this couple jokingly turned the conversation toward their sex life. Some private details were made awkwardly known as she poked some fun at her husband. Not only was this terribly awkward dinner conversation in mixed company, as it made everyone uncomfortable, but it obviously attacked the privacy and dignity of this woman's husband.

Both Donna and myself have made this same mistake in the past in ways not having to do with intimacy. We have both made jokes at each other's expense in mixed company from time to time that have been a bit personal in nature. We have both learned that making jokes in mixed company at each other's expense by spotlighting times when we have acted less than honorable is embarrassing to both her and me. Everyone knows that we all err in judgment from time to time, but no one likes to have their mistakes broadcast. After embarrassing one another several times by doing this, we have both learned to build each other up and praise one another in mixed company, not to make each other the brunt of jokes. Granted, there are certainly times when a couple who loves one another can have some fun and poke at each other, but when it starts getting personal, that's where the line is for Donna and me.

Everyone is born insecure because of the influence of sin, and if you can make it your life's mission to help people feel better about themselves, especially your spouse, then by the law of sowing and reaping you will naturally feel better about yourself, too.

"Do not be deceived: God is not mocked, for whatever one sows, that will he also reap."
–Galatians 6:7 (NIV)

"Finally, all of you, be like-minded, be sympathetic, love one another, be compassionate and humble. Do not repay evil with evil or insult with insult. On the contrary, repay evil with blessing, because to this you were called so that you may inherit a blessing."

-1 Peter 3:8-9 (NIV)

"Better to live on a corner of the roof than share a house with a quarrelsome wife."

-Proverbs 25:24 (NIV)

"Husbands, in the same way be considerate as you live with your wives, and treat them with respect as the weaker partner and as heirs with you of the gracious gift of life, so that nothing will hinder your prayers."

-1 Peter 3:7 (NIV)

"Love doesn't just sit there, like a stone, it has to be made, like bread; remade all the time, made new."

-Ursula K. Le Guin, The Lathe of Heaven

5

The Legacy of the Richest
Man Who Ever Lived

Steve lost nine jobs in his first six years after college. He was diagnosed a hopeless failure in business. But on his tenth job something happened. He went from earning less than half of the income of the average American during the first nine jobs to building a dozen multi-million dollar businesses from scratch, achieving sales of billions of dollars.

What happened?

One day during his years as a financial train wreck, a friend and mentor challenged Steve to study the book of Proverbs every day, promising that in doing so he would achieve greater success and happiness than he had ever known. Steve took that challenge, and in a relatively short period of time he became a millionaire many times over, and later authored a national bestseller entitled, *The Richest Man Who Ever Lived: King Solomon's Secrets to Success, Wealth, and Happiness.* That book has now even made its way into the hands of famous people in the secular world of business.

What Steven K. Scott discovered and later wrote about in his best-selling book are really not "secrets" at all, because they lie within the pages of Holy Scripture. But they *are* secrets in the sense that they remain undiscovered by the masses simply because the masses do not see the Bible as a handbook for success. How the Bible has been relegated to a book dealing exclusively with spiritual issues seems like the bigger mystery to me, because it is inundated with exhortations to study it for the monetary, social, and relational benefits it can bring. Yet this fact remains largely ignored or worse yet vilified by most churches, and is appears totally unknown to those outside the faith.

Some of the lengthiest passages in the Bible on any one subject have to do with gaining wisdom. The Bible clearly, strongly, and repeatedly encourages God's people to pursue wisdom, as wisdom is described as the *principle thing* in being good at life. The book of Proverbs from beginning to end is a continual declaration of the virtues of wisdom and sound judgment, and how they benefit one's life. One short but powerful example is found in Proverbs 24:5:

> *A wise man is full of strength, and a man of knowledge enhances his might.*
> *-Proverbs 24:5* (ESV)

What is Wisdom?

The definition of wisdom can be summed up simply with the understanding that it begins with the fear, or reverential awe and respect, of the Lord. The fear of the Lord flourishes in a heart that is humble. To fear the Lord simply means to hate evil, according to Proverbs 8:13. It is the fool who rejects God and His ways, but a person who is humble enough to submit to his Maker and love what He loves and hate what He hates is already on the road to wisdom.

> *And unto man he said, Behold, the FEAR OF THE LORD, that is wisdom; and to depart from evil is understanding."*
> *-Job 28:28* (KJV)

The FEAR OF THE LORD is the beginning of wisdom: a good understanding have all they that do his commandments: His praise endureth forever."
     -Psalm 111:10 (KJV)

The FEAR OF THE LORD is the beginning of wisdom: and the knowledge of the holy one is understanding."
     -Proverbs 9:10 (KJV)

It must also be pointed out that *knowledge* is not necessarily the same as wisdom. There are millions of people who know a lot about a lot of things, but who possess very little wisdom in which to apply that knowledge. We could say, therefore, that wisdom is the proper discernment and appropriate application of knowledge.

For example, I have known people who are very well informed about social, political, or religious issues, and who possess a lot of insight along those lines. In their attempts to educate others, however, they have so offended their peers in the fashion they have communicated those truths that they have failed in winning people over to their side, and, in fact, have made enemies. In other words, they possess knowledge, but not wisdom.

How to Obtain Wisdom

The starting place in obtaining wisdom has already been mentioned, and it is the fear of the Lord. The outflow of the fear of the Lord is self-reflection and self-examination. It is this introspection that allows one to learn wisdom from one's own mistakes.

I have made miserably stupid mistakes that were painful enough that they left indelible imprints on me. As a result, I learned from those mistakes. In other words, those mistakes gave me knowledge in certain situations that resulted in wisdom, or the ability to make good decisions and not bad ones.

Knowledge that results in wisdom can also be attained from watching the lives of others and observing what actions and decisions lead to broken lives, and likewise observing actions and decisions that lead to happiness and success.

Of course, knowledge and wisdom can also be attained from being a person who reads. Reading not only the Bible, but other developmental books and materials, listening to audio books and audio teachings, and reading biographies of great, accomplished and godly people can likewise be extremely helpful. This will exercise your mind and expand your intelligence. Being an avid reader of enriching material is one the most important things you will ever do to develop yourself.

Furthermore, knowledge and wisdom can also be attained by listening to advice and accepting instruction, a point I address in more detail in the following chapter.

The principle of pursuing wisdom and knowledge is so important that the scriptures say to do all you can do obtain wisdom, even if it costs you everything you have, because wisdom is the principle thing. Wisdom will exalt you. Wisdom will set a grand course for your life that is unobtainable otherwise. And when you obtain knowledge and wisdom, it is then your responsibility to do good with it and pass it on to others.

"Do not forsake wisdom, and she will protect you; love her, and she will watch over you. ...Get wisdom. Though it cost all you have, get understanding. Cherish her, and she will exalt you; embrace her, and she will honor you. She will give you a garland to grace your head and present you with a glorious crown."
–Proverbs 4:6-9n (NIV)

"Wisdom is not a product of schooling but of the lifelong attempt to acquire it."
-Albert Einstein

"In vain have you acquired knowledge if you have not imparted it to others."
-Deuteronomy Rabbah, Commentary on the Book of Deuteronomy

"An investment in knowledge always pays the best interest."
-Benjamin Franklin

"Knowledge rests not upon truth alone, but upon error also."
-Carl Jung

"A man can only attain knowledge with the help of those who possess it. This must be understood from the very beginning. One must learn from him who knows."
-George Ivanovich Gurdjieff

6

The Ballad of Richard Nixon

Former President Richard Nixon was a leader who made a habit of listening to and heeding the advice of his counselors. Perhaps his willingness to take advice so readily was learned the hard way when, during his first presidential campaign, he rejected the counsel of Dwight D. Eisenhower regarding debating his opponent, John F. Kennedy. Otto Friedrich wrote about the historic mistake in *Time* magazine:

> "Eisenhower and others warned Nixon not to accept Kennedy's challenge to a televised debate – Nixon was Vice President, after all, and far better known than the junior senator from Massachusetts – but Nixon took pride in his long experience as a debater. He also ignored advice to rest up for the debate and went on campaigning strenuously until the last minute. So, what a record 80 million Americans saw on their TV screens was a devastating contrast. Kennedy looked fresh, tanned, vibrant; Nixon looked unshaven, baggy-eyed, surly. The era of the politics of TV imagery

had begun, and the debates were a major victory
for Kennedy."

Kennedy, of course, went on to defeat Nixon by a razor-thin
margin, winning 50.4 percent of the popular vote and Nixon
winning 49.6 percent. Most analysts agree that if it had not been
for the televised debate, the tables would have turned and Nixon
would have easily won.

The principle of being teachable and accepting instruction does
not apply only to one's elders, coaches, or paid advisors, however.
A truly teachable person is open to any sort of instruction from
any source, young or old. While it is certainly true that not every
piece of advice is helpful, and not every criticism will be valid, a
teachable person is nevertheless willing to at least listen and then
carefully consider whatever criticism or advice is offered.

The Biblical mandate here is simple and straightforward. The
book of Proverbs is full of many different exhortations to accept
instruction, one of which is given in chapter 19:

> *"Listen to advice and accept instruction, that*
> *you may gain wisdom in the future."*
> *-Proverbs 19:20* (ESV)

The book of Proverbs also addresses those who make a habit
of rejecting advice, and it uses some of the Bible's strongest
language when describing them.

> *"Whoever loves discipline loves knowledge, but*
> *whoever hates correction is stupid."*
> *-Proverbs 12:1* (NIV)

The Bible does not mince words when it comes to describing
people who hate correction and refuse advice. It describes them
as fools because they don't understand that they are short-
circuiting their own progress. Their pride is killing them, and they

don't even know it. Rather than accepting advice graciously, they bristle and stiffen themselves. The Bible calls that being "stiff-necked." It's a dangerous position to be in, because those who are stiff-necked are being set up for disaster. They don't see that they are driving at high speed toward the edge of a cliff where calamity awaits them. Sometimes it takes a while to reach the edge of that cliff, but it's coming. Life is going to slap them upside the head, and when it does, very few recognize that they got themselves in the mess they are in. They blame other people; they blame their parents; they blame the government; they blame their husbands or wives; they blame their bosses; they blame everyone but themselves. And because they pass blame instead of examining themselves, they are destined to repeat the same cycle.

Why do people not like to listen to advice and accept instruction? There is only one answer to that question, and it all comes down to *pride*. To listen to advice, we have to admit to ourselves there is something we do not know. Accepting instruction means we have to acknowledge that perhaps we have made some wrong choices. To heed words of correction we have to recognize that someone knows more about something than we do and concede that perhaps we have acted foolishly in some respects. Those are things that most people are simply not willing to face, and that's why most people don't grow.

What I'm talking about here is a way of life unknown to the masses. Some success gurus and authors suggest that roughly ninety-eight percent of people go with the flow and do what everyone else does. According to these sources, it's only the top two percent of people who are the real movers and shakers in life,[1] and incidentally it is that top two percent who are usually willing to not only consider advice when it is offered, but they actually seek it out in many cases because they know that what they currently know is not all there is to know. It is this two percent who actually appreciates being corrected and are willing to contemplate even a harsh rebuke if it will lead to personal growth. That's why many of the most successful people in business, the arts, ministry, etc., will actually seek out a mentor or a personal coach of some sort.

Do you know some wise people, those who are older and more experienced than you? Good! Seek out their advice, and don't be afraid to accept instruction even if the form of correction or a rebuke. It's good for you! Not every piece of advice is always good advice, of course, and that's why the Bible also teaches that victory is found in *many* advisors. You have to look for answers in many different places and weigh what you hear against the direction of the Holy Spirit and guidance of the Scriptures. In doing so, you are more likely to avoid harm and arrive at a good place of peace and blessing.

"Whoever remains stiff-necked after many rebukes will suddenly be destroyed--without remedy."
-**Proverbs 29:1** (NIV)

"Those who disregard discipline despise themselves, but the one who heeds correction gains understanding."
-**Proverbs 15:32 9** (NIV)

"We give advice by the bucket, but take it by the grain."
-**William Alger**

"The two quickest ways to disaster are to take nobody's advice, and to take everybody's advice."
-**Unknown**

Reference:

1. The Top 2%: What it Takes to Reach the Top in Your Profession, *Nightingale Conant*, 2012, Simple Truths, LLC/ Nightingale-Conant

7

Finding Common Ground

Benjamin Franklin was a great statesmen and diplomat in early America. But he was not always skilled in the fine art of diplomacy. When he was a young man, his intelligence and wit were often on display at the expense of others. His turning point was when a trusted friend pulled him aside and gave him a sharp rebuke. "Ben, you are impossible," he said. "Your opinions have a slap in them for everyone who disagrees with you, and people find they enjoy themselves more when you are not around." To Franklin's credit, he received that rebuke, and used it to help him forge a great deal of skill as an ambassador, diplomat, and gentleman.

There are many lessons to be learned from the remarkable life of Benjamin Franklin. In this particular case, the story of the transformation of his social skills teaches us that there are ways to disagree without being disagreeable, the first rule of which is to choose your battles wisely. You don't always need to add your opinion to every conversation. In fact, people who feel the need to insert their views in every conversation are the kind of people that young Benjamin Franklin was. Some of these opinionated people may be quite intelligent and very well informed, but their bloated egos make them the brunt of jokes when out of earshot. Sometimes it is the best policy to simply let a sleeping dog lie. If someone is wrong about something, why be the one to always point it out? Why be "that guy?" Just let it go. You'll be happier, and so will the people around you.

In short, *try to find common ground with people. Try to focus on the things that you can agree with people about, not the things on which you disagree. Endeavor to be an agreeable person, not a disagreeable one.*

Some people seem to believe that it is their God-given obligation to be the world's "fact police," as I like to call it. But let me state a universal truth as clearly as I know how:

NO ONE LIKES A KNOW-IT-ALL WHO IS ALWAYS CORRECTING PEOPLE AND WHO MAKES HIMSELF OR HERSELF DISAGREEABLE FOR THE SAKE OF SHOWING OFF HIS OR HER KNOWLEDGE.

People who see themselves as fact police will eventually trim their list of friends down to a very small few by running off people who find them intolerable. Know-it-alls may be good at facts and information, but they are not very good at life. They don't make good friends. Therefore, the words of Proverbs 12:23 should be our guide:

> *The prudent keep their knowledge to themselves,*
> *but a fool's heart blurts out folly.*

I have had my share of unpleasant experiences with rude know-it-alls, and these experiences have increased with the growth of social media and digital communication. It seems that the lines of personal barriers and laws of social etiquette are blurred on social media, and people are all-too eager to insert their opinions in conversations where their opinions were not invited. Since I am a person with strong opinions myself, I have on occasion allowed myself to get sucked into arguments on social media where I found myself getting dragged down to the level of the first offender, and then becoming an offender myself!

On a side note, I am learning to heed the words of Mark Twain when it comes to debating with certain people: "Never argue with stupid people," he said. "They will drag you down to their level and then beat you on experience." I might insert the word *combative* in place of *stupid*, but either way, this is sage advice.

I have known people who truly do have great insight on certain matters, but they are unmannerly and sometimes downright bullies in offering their views. They barge into conversations where they were not invited, and then proceed to mop the floor with those whose opinions they desire to change. What do you think that kind of approach does to the recipient? Does it make him or her think better of the know-it-all? Does it make him or her feel impressed with the know-it-all's knowledge? No. In fact, just the opposite will occur. In my case, I have had to put some distance between myself and certain people who have made a habit of doing this sort of thing; not out of spite, but out of a desire to preserve my sense of serenity and sanity. No one needs to entertain toxic trouble-makers. In fact, Proverbs instructs,

> **"Throw out the mocker and out goes strife;**
> **quarrels and insults are ended."**
> **-Proverbs 22:10** (NIV)

Sadly, some people who make a habit of taking the charging bull approach to disagreements do it over issues that are sometimes very insignificant. Some people have no idea how to wisely choose their battles. And once a person is deeply offended it is very difficult to win them back. As Proverbs 18:19 says,

> **"An offended friend is harder to win back than a**
> **fortified city. Arguments separate friends like a gate**
> **locked with bars."** (NLT)

It is very unfortunate that friendships have been strained and even lost over issues that don't really matter.

On the other hand, there are indeed certain issues on which you will need to firmly take a stand. While you will not always win over your opponent on every issue, you certainly have a better chance of it when you are agreeable on most other issues, and when you are diplomatic about the ones on which you disagree. My mother taught me a saying along these lines that stuck with me: "You catch more flies using honey than vinegar." That is very true.

The best way to have a conversation with someone when exchanging different viewpoints is to first try to understand the other person's argument. Show genuine interest in his or her opinion, and listen intently so that you can thoroughly understand what you are arguing against, and also so you can extend respect. If you are a good listener, you will have a better chance of gaining the mutual respect of your opponent.

Next, do not offer your views dogmatically. Dogmatic people look foolish when they sometimes have to eat their words on the occasions that they are proven wrong. So leave room to be proven wrong, because, who knows; *you might be.*

Open your comments by first asking for permission to offer a different viewpoint and acknowledging the fact that you might actually be wrong, something like this: *"Those are some very good points. I really like how you have thought this through, and I understand what you are saying. I have some thoughts along these lines, too, that might not be exactly right; after all, I've been wrong more times that I can count. But may I offer this view for the sake of discussion?"*

Who is going to get agitated over an opening like that? It is not condescending, it's not combative, and it's not disrespectful. In fact, it's inviting. Most people would be happy to give a hearing to someone who shows that kind of respect. What people *will* react to, however, is if you open your argument by saying, "That's ridiculous," or "You're just wrong," or the clever but rude put-down I have heard used by even ministers, "I would agree with you but then we would both be wrong." That is the best way to get a reaction that you won't like.

Another lesson I have learned – the hard way, I might add – is that confrontations and disagreements should be done face-to-face or over the phone if possible, not in writing. I am amazed at how people will read into letters or emails things that are not there; a point also related to my experiences on social media.

I confronted a lady in our church a few years ago about something that she had done that was clearly inappropriate and damaging to our fellowship. I thought I was fine to do it in writing because the words of instruction were very brief and gentle, and cushioned on both ends with copious amounts of compliments. The correction was maybe three sentences worded very carefully stuck in the middle of an email that was dripping with praise for her. I honestly expected her to read that email feeling better about herself. But that's not what happened. She had an emotional meltdown. Very unlike Benjamin Franklin's response to his friend's rebuke, this lady rejected the correction, took it as an insult, and made such a huge issue over it that I had to have a meeting with her and her husband and four other leaders from our church to try to get it straightened out, and they *still* left our church. The lady's response was so extreme that I doubt a face-to-face confrontation would have been much better, but nevertheless a face-to-face conversation would have allowed her to see my facial expressions and hear my tone of voice, and maybe, just maybe, that might have prevented her from entertaining vain imaginations.

Another thing I have observed about written communication is how many liberties people take with their own writing. People are emboldened behind the safety of their keyboards and will say things that they would never say to someone in person. Facebook, in particular, has become a hive of hateful words thrown around very recklessly.

Take a word of advice from someone who has foolishly learned many of my lessons the hard way: Don't allow someone to draw you into a written argument with their combative words. If a text, email, or social media conversation starts to get heated, cut if off, or perhaps suggest to the person on the other end that maybe the two of you should meet for coffee and discuss further. Even if someone accuses you of something and you feel a surge of energy to defend yourself, best not to do it in writing, unless, of course, you are an extremely restrained person and very skilled in written communication. But even if you are very skilled in written communication, the truth remains that people are emboldened behind the safety of their impersonal keyboards, and are less restrained as a result. Thus, it might be best to respond something like this: "I understand your concerns and I would be very happy to address them. Let's meet for lunch and discuss. What is the best time to get together?" If a person refuses an invitation like that, then they are not really after a resolution to the situation anyway; they just want to fight.

The bottom line is that you will *never* win anyone over to your side by being condescending, patronizing, or combative – which is also a word to the wise for husbands and wives, by the way. Know-it-alls may win a lot of arguments, but they don't win many friends. The best policy is to try to find common ground with people and emphasize the issues on which you agree. In the event that you must hash out a disagreement, then heed the words of scripture by using gentle, diplomatic words, and *that* is the way to promote instruction and increase your persuasiveness.

"The wise of heart is called discerning, and sweetness of speech increases persuasiveness."
-Proverbs 16:21 (NIV)

"Kindness makes a person attractive. If you want to win the world, melt it, do no hammer it."
- Alexander MacLaren

"Truth without love is brutality."
-Warren W. Wiersbe

"Tact is the knack of making a point without making an enemy."
-Isaac Newton

"A gentle answer deflects anger, but harsh words make tempers flare."
-Proverbs 15:1 (NLT)

"The supreme art of war is to subdue the enemy without fighting."
-Sun Tzu, The Art of War

"Force is all conquering, but its victories are short lived."
-Abraham Lincoln

"Death and life are in the power of the tongue."
-Proverbs 18:21 (ESV)

8

Like Falling off a Slippery Log

During the days of the human rights movement of the 1960s when black Americans were rising up against terrible prejudices and injustices, the foremost leader of that movement, Dr. Martin Luther King, Jr, had every right, humanly speaking, to hate and revile. Yet, it was this man whose life was threatened numerous times and who did eventually pay the ultimate price, who said, "I have decided to stick with love; hate is too great a burden to bear."

It takes a very strong person to love the haters and mockers. It is the easiest thing in the world to hate people who wrong you, who do not live up to your standards, who are prideful, hateful, ignorant, and prejudiced. Hate is like falling off a slippery log. It takes no effort at all. It is the sinful nature's default position. Anyone can hate! But love takes effort in many cases, especially love that stands the test of time. That's why Jesus said,

> [32]*"If you love those who love you, what credit is that to you? Even sinners love those who love them.* [33]*And if you do good to those who are good to you, what credit is that to you? Even sinners do that.* [34]*And if you lend to those from whom you expect*

repayment, what credit is that to you? Even sinners lend to sinners, expecting to be repaid in full. ³⁵But love your enemies, do good to them, and lend to them without expecting to get anything back. Then your reward will be great, and you will be children of the Most High..."
      -Luke 6:32-35 (NIV)

To demonstrate the fallen nature of mankind, think about the last time you had a knee-jerk reaction of loving feelings toward someone who severely wronged you or who acts ungrateful or unloving? That's not the way human nature works. It takes effort to push past the natural reactions of the fallen human nature in order to get to the love that God has placed in the hearts of all who call on His Name. And when I say effort, loving someone who doesn't deserve it can be the the most difficult thing you've ever tried to do. But doing so is acting like our Savior, Who first loved us when we did not deserve it, and Who continues to do so through our selfishness, rebellion, and stupidity. He is patient with the process, and He commands that we do the same for others who are not as far along as we have come.

In being patient with people who are in process, we must not only reserve judgment for God to mete out, but we must also refrain from reviling, condemning, or deriding our neighbors. Weak people hate and revile, but strong people love and build up.

We must understand that love is not necessarily an emotion, and it's not just *saying* you love someone or refusing to revile a person. Love demonstrates itself in doing and not just saying; in reaching out to others; yes, even our enemies, because to once again quote Dr. Martin Luther King, Jr., "Love is the only thing that can transform an enemy into a friend."

No Better than a Whore

In First Corinthians 13, the famous "love chapter" of the Bible, there is a cultural perspective often missed by modern readers.

Verse one says that if we don't have love, we are as "sounding brass or a tinkling cymbal." Most people interpret that to mean that if we don't have love, all of our other good deeds are just noise-making and have no real value. While I do believe that is an accurate perspective, there is more to that phrase that finds its fuller meaning in the culture of the day.

The book of First Corinthians was penned by the Apostle Paul and was addressed to the Christians of the city of Corinth. Corinth was a culture thoroughly immersed in paganism. They worshiped many gods, one of which was Aphrodite, the "goddess of love." The worship of Aphrodite included temple prostitution, and every female who took part in that perverse religion was to serve a rotation periodically as a temple prostitute. From the wife and daughters of the highest official, to the lowest vagrant, every female in a household who worshiped Aphrodite was required to do her duty.

Temple prostitutes in Corinth would advertise their availability in two ways: they would cut their hair short, and they would wear bells or tiny cymbals around their ankles. The cutting of their hair, by the way, is one of the reasons why the Apostle Paul instructed the female Christians in Corinth to refrain from cutting their hair short. He did not want Christ followers to be confused or associated with prostitution. The wearing of the ankle cymbals among temple prostitutes likewise shines an important light on Paul's statement in First Corinthians 13:1. Everyone reading those words who lived in Corinth understood the reference loud and clear. **Paul was literally saying that if a person doesn't have love, he or she is no better than a whore.** According to Paul's graphic reference, a Christian who does not strive toward the love of Christ being demonstrated in his or her life is like a cheap temple prostitute who observes religious ritual but who degrades and defiles herself in the process.

As stated already, love is not simply an emotion. Biblical love, in fact, will often ignore emotion in order to demonstrate the love of Christ. This kind of *agape'* love – the kind that only God can give – has specific characteristics, and the standards are high. We find that list in the love chapter, First Corinthians 13:4-7:

> **⁴Love is patient and kind. Love is not jealous or boastful or proud ⁵or rude. It does not demand its own way. It is not irritable, and it keeps no record of being wronged. ⁶It does not rejoice about injustice but rejoices whenever the truth wins out. ⁷Love never gives up, never loses faith, is always hopeful, and endures through every circumstance.** (NLT)

So we see that the God-kind of love is not always thinking about self-preservation or self-interest or self-promotion, but demonstrates itself in a selfless kind of expression that places others above itself. Humanly speaking, this is extremely difficult, if not impossible, especially as it pertains to those who are not so easy to love. That is precisely why we need to seek God's strength to love like this. Selfish human interest cannot love like this, which is why I said in the opening statements of this chapter that loving others and building them up is the high road that requires an enormous amount of God-given strength, whereas hating and reviling others is the position of the weak. And that's why Jesus said in Luke 6 that *anyone* can love those who are easy to love; the worst of sinners can do that! But His mandate is to love the unlovely just as Jesus has loved us, to forgive the unforgivable just as we have been forgiven, and to refrain from judging so that we can avoid judgment.

While learning to love according to the standards of First Corinthians 13 is a tall order, it nevertheless represents a standard of how to be good at life. You see, hate begets more hate, whereas love promotes more love and brings good things into one's life. Even irreligious people understand the Biblical concept of sowing and reaping, a concept sometimes referred to as "karma" by some people not familiar with the Biblical origin. The truth of Galatians 6:7, that whatsoever people sow is the same thing they will ultimately reap, is nearly a universally understood concept, even if it is not acknowledged as a Biblical truth. If you sow hatefulness, judgment, and reviling toward people, that's the same thing you will reap back in time after the seeds you have planted sprout and grow. You may not see it overnight, but it's coming. If you sow love, mercy, and patience toward people, that, too, is what you will reap. Choosing the latter is a big part of what it means to be good at life.

"Dear children, let us not love with words or speech but with actions and in truth."
-1 John 3:18 (NIV)

[14] *"We know that we have passed from death to life, because we love each other. Anyone who does not love remains in death. [15]Anyone who hates a brother or sister is a murderer, and you know that no murderer has eternal life residing in him."*
-1 John 3:14-15 (NIV)

[27] *"But to you who are listening I say: Love your enemies, do good to those who hate you, [28]bless those who curse you, pray for those who mistreat you. [29]If someone slaps you on one cheek, turn to them the other also. If someone takes your coat, do not withhold your shirt from them. [30]Give to everyone who asks you, and if anyone takes what belongs to you, do not demand it back. [31]Do to others as you would have them do to you."*
-Luke 6:27-31 (NIV)

"Love is when the other person's happiness is more important than your own."
–H. Jackson Brown Jr.

"Whoever belittles his neighbor lacks sense, but a man of understanding remains silent."
-Proverbs 11:12 (ESV)

9

Sins Against Nature

Hippocrates said, *"Illnesses to do not come upon us out of the blue. They are developed from small daily sins against nature. When enough sins have accumulated, illness will suddenly appear."*

The above Hippocrates quote is generally true. I must add, however, that sometimes people do get ill because of genetic issues that they cannot control. Even so, the Surgeon General once proclaimed that 7 out of 10 of the most common causes of death in America are diet and lifestyle related. In other words, the way people eat is often killing them. Any discussion on being good at life would not be complete without a short discussion about food, because food is the fuel of life.

Food is more than just calories. Food is *information* – information to your cells. Like the programming of a computer, food tells your body how to function. The consumption of food produces chemical messengers in the body called, *kinases*. There are certain kinases that respond to high quality nutrition-packed foods and send messages of health and strength throughout the body. There are other types of kinases that respond to low-quality foods by sending alarm molecules throughout the body that create inflammation, tissue damage, and degeneration.

Thus, medical science has proven that the quality of food you eat determines how your body will function.

Medical science has also confirmed that what you put into your body can positively or negatively affect how your brain functions, which pertains not only to your cognitive skills, but also your mood. This is part of the reason why God gave the ancient Israelites strict instructions regarding their food and what was "clean" and "unclean." God commanded clean eating and good hygiene in the Old Testament not only for symbolic and ceremonial functions, but also for the purpose of vibrant health and avoiding many of the maladies that plagued the nations where clean eating was not adhered to. While we in the New Covenant age are free from the ceremonial obligations of the Old Testament Law regarding food and hygiene, the health principles are timeless.

For example, God's laws for hygiene in the Old Testament were very strict and applied to practically everything related to the spread of germs. As a result, the Jews did not suffer diseases of contagion to the extent of the neighboring nations. Even centuries later when the "Black Death" plague swept over Europe in the 14th Century and wiped out an estimated 75 million people, it is fascinating to note that Jewish communities were hardly affected. That contagious plague was one caused by poor hygiene, but the Jews in the 14th Century were still adhering to strict Old Testament laws of diet and hygiene. So effective were their methods in protecting them from these contagious diseases to which everyone else around them seemed to be falling victim, some people actually believed that the Jews were the cause of the plagues.

(On a side note, germs were not discovered until around 1860. Yet the laws of hygiene included in the Levitical Law passed down to Moses from God were written thousands of years ago when some people groups were still using dung in their medical prescriptions. The wisdom of the Bible is timeless.)

Similarly, we now know that shellfish, which was forbidden

in the Old Testament Law, is much more allergenic compared to "clean" fish. Allergies to shellfish are fairly common, whereas allergies to fatty fish like tuna and salmon are far less so. While people in the New Testament age are not sinning if they eat shellfish since God's people are no longer obligated to those ceremonial laws, certain foods nevertheless have health risks associated with their consumption.

While I am not promoting strict adherence to Jewish Old Testament Law since our salvation does not rest on that, my point is that some people seem to believe that God couldn't care less how we take care of our bodies, but that obviously isn't true. God was as much interested in the health, vitality, and long life of His people as He was the ceremonial purposes behind the Law, because He loves His people and wants us to prosper. *"Beloved, I pray that in all respects you may prosper and be in good health, just as your soul prospers"* (3 John 1:2). God said of Himself in Malachi 3:6, *"I am the LORD; I do not change."* He is just as much interested in the health of His people today as He was during the days of Mosaic Law.

Nearly every sports coach and business success guru will teach least some information on the importance of healthy lifestyles. You cannot perform at your best if you are not feeding your body the best. The late motivational speaker and author, Zig Ziglar, for example, frequently gave mention to the importance of healthy eating in order to keep one's energy, mood, and daily performance on a consistently high level. In his audio series, *Raising Positive Kids in a Negative World*, Ziglar also went into detail about how parents should prioritize clean eating for their children to aid them in controlling their moods and emotions.

Food choices affect more than one's mood, however. In ancient times there were maladies known as "the diseases of kings and queens," so named because these diseases affected mostly wealthy people who ate very rich diets. These maladies were lifestyle diseases such as heart disease, obesity, tumors, fatigue, depression, and chronic pain. The commoners of the day did not suffer such problems for the most part. What was the difference? Their diets! The wealthy people of the day ate lots of meat, sweetened and refined carbohydrates (sugary, processed foods), and drank lots of alcohol (also processed). Commoners consumed moderate amounts of meat that they mostly raised and prepared themselves, and lots of fruits and vegetables and whole grains that they raised themselves.

Today, Americans live in a culture with a nearly endless food supply. Choices abound. We are a nation of "kings and queens." Thus, the diseases of kings and queens that are preventable are the most common scourges of our time. As mentioned already, it is telling that the Surgeon General, in fact, stated that seven out of ten of the leading killers in America are *lifestyle diseases* that are linked to diet and lifestyle. Seven out of ten!

There is a profound passage in the book of Proverbs that speaks to this.

> **¹"When you sit to dine with a ruler, note well what is set before you, and put a knife to your throat if you are given to gluttony. ²Do not crave his delicacies, for that food is deceptive."**
> **–Proverbs 23:1-2** (NIV)

This passage was written by King Solomon of ancient Israel approximately 4,000 years ago when diseases linked to excess and poor food choices became associated with affluence. Solomon was passing on a nugget of sage wisdom regarding food and health, saying that it is not wise to crave the rich food of rulers and dignitaries. Notice that he says to "note well what is set before" if you happen to be the dinner guest of a ruler. He goes on to say that that food is "deceptive." What is deceptive food? Deceptive food looks good, tastes good, smells good, but it definitely not good *for* you.

The effect of food was also demonstrated clearly in the book of Daniel. In chapter one, young Daniel and his friends, Hananiah,

Mishael and Azaria, were taken into exile in Babylon along with thousands of other Israelites. Even though in exile, God's favor nevertheless rested on these faithful young men, and they were treated well and taken into the service of the Babylonian king. All who were taken into the king's service were given the king's royal food, which included many things that were considered unclean by any Israelite who was following the Mosaic Law. Daniel therefore made a proposition to the king's chief official as a way to avoid eating the king's unclean food.

> "⁸*But Daniel resolved not to defile himself with the royal food and wine, and he asked the chief official for permission not to defile himself this way... ¹¹Daniel then said to the guard whom the chief official had appointed over Daniel, Hananiah, Mishael and Azariah, ¹² 'Please test your servants for ten days: Give us nothing but vegetables to eat and water to drink. ¹³Then compare our appearance with that of the young men who eat the royal food, and treat your servants in accordance with what you see.' ¹⁴So he agreed to this and tested them for ten days. ¹⁵At the end of the ten days they looked healthier and better nourished than any of the young men who ate the royal food. ¹⁶So the guard took away their choice food and the wine they were to drink and gave them vegetables instead.*"
> -*Daniel 1:8-16* (NIV)

From the perspectives of both medical science and the Bible, then, food choices can clearly lead a person toward or away from vibrant health eventually. And vibrant health buys what money cannot. A person can be rich financially, but if they are chronically sick or have low energy, they would often give all they have to feel good again. A healthy body is a *happy* body.

While a young person can get away with bad eating habits for many years in some cases, eventually their bad habits catch up with them. They reap what they sow in time. Like a smoker who enjoys his habit for many years without any visible ill effects but then is "suddenly" diagnosed with lung cancer or emphysema, eating poor quality food as a matter of lifestyle will more often than not eventually reap consequences as well, ranging from minor to terminal.

At the time of this writing I have been a consultant for nearly 24 years to hundreds of holistic and integrative health professionals. Integrative and holistic practitioners seek to discover the root of disease and dysfunction rather than just chasing symptoms with drugs. Drugs and surgery have their place, but I have not met a doctor yet who believes that the root of disease is a drug deficiency. While there are genetics, stress, and other factors to consider, the fact is that 100% of the holistic and integrative medical professionals I am privileged to know agree that most of the time it is a person's lifestyle that leads to breakdowns in health. For this reason, dietary changes are always part of the protocol for getting back to good health under the care of an integrative health professional, and is also given at least lip service by even most conventional medical professionals. Therefore, the larger part of treating one's body well and regaining vibrant health is making smart food choices.

If you think about it, eating right for optimal cognitive and physical performance just makes sense. Consider how a car functions, for example. When I bought my first car that was designed to run on high-octane fuel, I found out quickly that putting cheaper fuel in the car may have saved me a few bucks on the front end, but it cost me on the back end in terms of my car's performance. Putting low octane gasoline in an automobile that requires high octane fuel will often cause the engine to sputter, smoke and knock, and the power of the car suffers. Using low-octane fuel often enough in a high-octane car will result in reducing the life of the engine as well.

If this is true with an automobile, how much more so

for something as complex and delicate as the human body! God designed the body to run on high-octane fuel, if you will, like vitamins, minerals, fatty acids, amino acids, complex carbohydrates, fiber, and clean water. Our Creator placed these fuel sources on our planet in the form of fruits, vegetables, nuts and grains for our enjoyment and vitality. To snub these foods is to snub His wisdom. Whenever mankind changes God's design we do so at a cost, and the cost in this case is the possibility of developing disease or dysfunction of some sort. I cannot count the times that I have met people who are sick with all manner of terrible health problems but who don't seem to make the connection that the way they eat is contributing to those maladies. "I don't like vegetables," is the mantra of many. But do you like good health? Often certain disciplines must be in place to enjoy the finer things of life, like vibrant health!

To illustrate the cost of circumventing God's creation, I am including here my own modified version of a clever illustrative story that appears online in several forms. I offer my updated version here to elucidate on the point.

"In the Beginning, Retold"

In the beginning, God created the Heavens and the Earth, and populated the ground with spinach, carrots and beets, and yellow, green, and red fruits and vegetables of all kinds, so that mankind would live long and strong.

Satan, however, perverted God's design and invented sugary ice cream and cream-filled donuts. And as Man and Woman gained 10 pounds, Satan smiled.

God then created whole oats, that Woman might keep the figure that Man found so fair. But Satan responded by bringing forth white flour from the wheat, and sugar from the cane and mingled them. And Woman went from size 6 to size 12.

So God said, "Behold, my fresh green salad." And Satan served up Thousand-Island dressing, buttery croutons and garlic toast on the side. And Man and Woman unfastened their belts to relieve the pressure from their gastric distress.

God then said, "I have sent you heart healthy vegetables and olive oil in which to cook them." And Satan conjured up deep-dish pizza and breaded fried chicken. And Man gained more weight, and his cholesterol spiked.

God then created light, fluffy rice cakes so that Man and Woman might reduce their weight, and He declared, "It is good." Satan then devised the chocolate cake and name it, "Devil's Food."

God then brought forth running shoes so that His children might burn extra calories and stave off disease. Behold, the crafty devil responded again by bringing forth the satellite TV with a remote control so Man would not have to toil changing the channels. And Man and Woman laughed and cried before the flickering light, and gained more pounds.

Then God brought forth the potato, naturally low in fat and brimming with nutrition. And Satan peeled off the healthful skin and sliced the starchy center into chips and deep-fried them. And Man and Woman again gained pounds, and their energy waned.

God then gave turkey and lean beef so that Man might consume fewer calories and still satisfy his appetite. But Satan created Burger King and said, "Have it your way!" Then Satan said, "Do you want fries with that?" And Man replied, "Yes! And a milk-shake, please!" And Satan said, "It is good." And Man went into cardiac arrest.

God sighed and created quadruple bypass surgery, holistic medicine, and vitamin supplements that man might regain his vigor.

Then Satan created Obamacare.

Clean eating, then, is not rocket science. One rule of thumb to keep in mind is simply eat mostly fresh plant foods in the form of a wide variety of vegetables, fruits, beans, and nuts, and buy organic if you can. Organic foods have not been adulterated with toxic chemical pesticides, herbicides, colorings, and antibiotics. When choosing meat, choose lean meats like chicken, turkey, lamb, deer and fish, with the smaller percentage of your meat consumption coming from more fatty meats like beef and pork. Make fried foods the exception and eat a majority of your food raw, boiled, steamed, or baked. As for sugary foods like sodas, candy, and desserts, keep these at a minimum, and make purified water your friend.

While there is much more to say about clean eating than this, these simple guidelines are a good starting place. You can always choose to educate yourself further on the subject if necessary. There is no shortage of excellent educational resources on habits for healthy living for those who want to learn more. I encourage this, as the lazy and sloppy lifestyle habits of most Americans is why 1 in 3 now die from heart disease,[1] why cancer is the second leading cause of death and kills more than a half million Americans every year,[2] and why 29 million Americans have diabetes,[3] a terrible lifestyle disease which raises the risk to heart disease and cancer even more.

To once again circle back around to an earlier point, your food choices can definitely also affect your mood and your cognitive performance, and thus possibly your career, relationships and enjoyment of life. As stated in the article in WebMD, *How Food Affects Your Moods*, "...the science of food's affect on mood is based on this: Dietary changes can bring about changes in our brain structure (chemically and physiologically), which can lead to altered behavior."[4]

Altered behavior? Yes, you read that correctly. Living off of nutritionally-flawed fast food and junk food, according to the research, can affect a person's judgment and behavior because it changes (damages) the function of the brain. This altered behavior and judgment may contribute to problems in school, on the job, in relationships, and in society.

Therefore, there are many reasons to make the best food choices that you can as often as you can. And that, too, is part of what it means to be good at life!

"Nearly all disease can be traced to a nutritional deficiency."
-Dr. Linus Pauling, two-time Nobel Prize winner

"Good nutrition, adequate sleep, and regular exercise are all it takes to stay healthy. [Pharmaceutical drugs] merely enable the delusion that one can cut corners on those three without consequence. If a child gets all three of those, he will never need to see the pediatrician. And if an adult gets all three, it is very likely that he will live a pain free, medicine free, and doctor free life!"
-Dr. Michael Cassaro, MD, Pain Specialist

"Let food be thy medicine and medicine be thy food."
-Hippocrates

"The food you eat can either be the safest and most powerful form of medicine, or the slowest form of poison."
    -Ann Wigmore

"When diet is wrong, medicine is of no use; when diet is correct, medicine is of no need."
    -Ayurvedic Proverb

"Just because you're not sick doesn't mean you're healthy."
    -Unknown

"The doctor of the future will give no medicine, but will instruct his patients in care of the human frame, in diet, and the cause and prevention of disease."
    -Thomas Edison

"I really regret eating healthy today."
    -Said No One Ever

References:
1. Heart Disease Now Kills 1 of every 3 Americans. *WebMD*, December 16, 2015
2. Cancer Statistics, *National Cancer Institute*, March 14, 2016
3. 2014 National Diabetes Report, *Centers for Disease Control and Prevention*, CDC.gov.
4. How Food Affects Your Moods, *WebMD*, Elaine Magee, MPH, RD, 2008

10

Honor Them, and God Will Honor You

There was a ruler in ancient Israel by the name of Rehoboam, a young know-it-all who resisted the wisdom of the aged. Rehoboam was the son of Solomon and grew up in privilege, and events would prove how prideful and self-absorbed he was. When Israel was preparing to make Rehoboam king after Solomon's death, representatives came to him with a question regarding how he would rule, because they were concerned about the harsh labor they had endured under King Solomon. They said, *"Your father put a heavy yoke on us, but now lighten the harsh labor and the heavy yoke he put on us, and we will serve you"* (1 Kings 12:4). Rehoboam responded by sending them away for three days so he could think about his answer. He consulted with two groups of advisors. One group of advisors was made up of friends who grew up with him, and the other was made up of aged, seasoned elders who had served King Solomon. The elders advised young Rehoboam to answer the people favorably, to serve them, and in response the people would gladly serve him. But this advice was not what proud and pugnacious Rehoboam wanted to hear. He decided to heed the advice of his contemporaries who urged him to establish his authority by answering the people harshly and threateningly, essentially throwing his weight around.

The result? The people rebelled against Rehoboam, and for the first time in Israel's history the kingdom was split, with Rehoboam losing 11 of the 12 tribes of Israel, ruling only over Judah. How differently history would have played out if only Rehoboam would have set aside his youthful pride and listened to his elders.

There is nothing quite so potentially exasperating to an older adult than the conduct of a very young know-it-all – a person who has not lived the length of time necessary to accumulate a true combination of both broad knowledge and deep wisdom, yet who behaves as though superior in knowledge to those who have lived twice as long or more.

At the same time, we must likewise acknowledge that age is certainly no guarantee of intelligence, godly character, or wisdom, that's for sure. Some people remain ignorant and self-centered all their lives. But young people would be well-advised to realize that they are at a distinct disadvantage when it comes to knowledge and wisdom compared to someone much older, and hence, their conduct toward their elders should be seasoned with the due honor.

For example, neuroscience has proven that the prefrontal cortex of the brain – the region involved in decision making and moderating social behavior – is not fully developed until age 25 or so. (Now I understand why I acted the way I did when I was in my 20s!) Think of it! Young adults often do not even have the neurological maturity that is needed to make the best choices and conduct themselves wisely some of the time. Yet many of these same young people behave as though they have already arrived at the pinnacle of wisdom and intelligence. It's not that a young adult is incapable of making wise choices and sound judgments. But there are certainly challenges along those lines to overcome.

Proverbs 20:29 tells us that *"The glory of the young is their strength; the gray hair of experience is the splendor of the old."* Yet the downfall of many young adults is that they are notorious for believing that they are the fount of knowledge and wisdom and the older people are foolish and out of touch. The wise young person will understand that he/she is not as smart as a lot of young people like to think. The older I have grown, in fact, the more I realize there is a universe of things I still don't know and the more I see how foolish I was when I was younger (and still am sometimes).

Understanding the deficiencies in neurochemistry and the lack of experience of youth should be sufficient motivation for young people to seek the counsel of godly and successful elders, but should also inspire the young person to seek God and the wisdom of His Word all the more.

The Special Blessing in Honoring Parents

The American society used to be one of great honor. Parents, elders, and overseers were honored in our society, and now people in positions of authority are commonly disparaged. Police officers are now even hated by a large segment of our society, the very ones who put their lives at stake to keep law, order, and peace. Sitcoms routinely cast the parents, and in particular fathers, as buffoons, and the children as the cool and insightful ones. Even pastors are depicted by Hollywood as corrupt and dishonest hypocrites. Thus, many of the young adults in Western society are infected with the disease of self-importance while demeaning the aged and those in authority.

While honoring all elders and people in authority is an important principle in being good at life, there is particular blessing in honoring one's parents according to Scripture. The twentieth chapter of Exodus lists God's sacred Ten Commandments, and the fifth commandment is a clear mandate to honor one's parents. This mandate is reiterated by the Apostle Paul in his letter to the Ephesian church, making it clear that this commandment is a standard by which the New Testament believer must still align one's self.

What is meant by "honor?" The Hebrew word translated into English as honor is *kabed* (pronounced, *kaw-bade*), which more literally means *to glorify, to promote, to boast, abounding with, to lay heavily, and to make weighty.* The latter three definitions of *kabed* are interesting in that they do not seem to fit with the first three. However, the connotation and usage of the word as it appears in Exodus 20:12 seems to suggest that the promotion and glorification of parents should be applied so liberally and generously that it actually becomes like pouring something onto someone or loading them down with something so thoroughly that there is absolutely no lack. Similarly, the definition *to make weighty* could also mean that the children bear a great weight of responsibility in carrying out the glorification of their parents as Biblically defined here.

For practical application of this mandate, let us refer to Matthew Henry's Complete Commentary on the Whole Bible. Below is his commentary on Exodus 20:12, edited slightly for clarity as to reflect modern day English.

> "The fifth commandment concerns duties we owe to our relations; specifically those of children to their parents: *Honor thy father and thy mother,* which includes,
>
> 1. A decent respect to their persons, an inward esteem of them outwardly expressed upon all occasions in our conduct toward them. *Fear* [show an awesome respect for] *them* (Leviticus 19:3), and *give them reverence* (Hebrews 12:9). The contrary to this is mocking at them and despising them (Proverbs 30:17).
>
> 2. Obedience to their lawful commands, as expounded upon in Ephesians 6:1-3; *Children obey your parents.* Come when they call you, go where they send you, do what they bid you, refrain from what they forbid you; and do this cheerfully in an attitude of love.

3. Submit to their rebukes, instructions, and corrections; and do this not only to the good and gentle parent, but also to the stubbornly contrary and disobedient parent, out of conscience toward God.

4. Inclining to their advice, direction, and consent, and seeking their approval.

5. Endeavoring in everything to be the comfort of their parents, and to make their old age easy to them, maintaining them as if they stand in need of support, which our Savior makes to be particularly intended in this commandment."

While this standard, no doubt, appears somewhat lofty for some, especially for those who are children of a "stubbornly contrary and disobedient" parent, it is not without benefit for those who observe these standards, as Ephesians 6:1-3 describes:

> *"Children, obey your parents in the Lord, for this is right. Honor your father and mother – which is the first commandment with a promise – 'that it may go well with you and that you may enjoy long life on the earth'."* (NIV)

We must be aware that no age is given in scripture for when a child is free from the obligation to honor his or her parents. As far as the reader of scripture can discern, God intends for children to honor and revere parents for a lifetime.

This presents, however, some troubling emotions for some. Honoring and revering parents who are abusive, self-centered, and anything but nurturing is usually the farthest thing from the minds of children who have been mistreated, unloved, or victimized by their parents. I have written an entire small book on this subject called, *Honor Your Father and Mother: A Biblical Perspective on What Parental Honor Really Means in Modern Times,* to help the reader understand how and why the scriptures mandate honoring even parents who are not honorable. Although I cannot unravel that issue here, I will bottom-line it by saying that while honoring dishonorable parents might not seem like an easy or even logical thing to do, God nevertheless makes an amazing promise to those who keep this mandate. He says to honor one's parents so that things may go well with you and that you may have a long life.

Let's get this straight. If I want things to go well with me and if I want to have a long life, all I have to do is honor my parents according to the Biblical standard? Well, yes. That *is* what the scriptures say. While there are certainly other principles to apply to one's life for living a happy, successful, and long life – which is the reason for this book – we certainly cannot overlook this principle. After all, I don't know of anywhere else in the Bible where God makes this kind of promise where He assures both a *long* and *good* life.

I have repeatedly witnessed in both my own life and among friends and acquaintances what a life of parental honor can result in versus what dishonoring one's parents does to people. Almost without exception, the people I know who have done a good job of honoring their parents are blessed people in almost every respect of their lives. Conversely, the people in my circle of acquaintances who have not honored their parents well are almost without exception cursed in some way: in their health, their finances, their relationships, their marriages, how their kids turned out, etc.

One of the more extreme examples of this is 1970s punk rocker, John Ritchie (alias: Sid Vicious), of the band, *The Sex Pistols*. Ritchie was an anarchist who raged against all authority. He once declared, "*Undermine their pompous authority, reject their moral standards, make anarchy and disorder your trademarks. Cause as much chaos and disruption as possible but don't let them take you ALIVE.*" And what was Ritchie's end? He was arrested for the stabbing murder of his girlfriend, Nancy Spungen, but before the case could be brought to trial, he died of a heroin overdose at the tender age of 21. As one of the most outspoken anarchists of modern culture, he is a vivid example of how the truth expressed in Ephesians 6:1-3 can work for or against a person.

What about In-Laws?

We must be aware that God's standards of honoring one's parents, and all elders for that matter, certainly extends to in-laws. For a husband to encourage in any way, even subtly, any degree of dishonor, disrespect, or diminishing of the relationship between his wife and her parents and extended family is tantamount to tempting her to sin. And the reverse is also true. For a wife to absorb her husband into her family at the expense of his relationships with his parents and siblings is terribly destructive and a leading of her spouse into sin.

I was brought up in a terribly dysfunctional family situation, and because of the pain I endured, I grew to become somewhat calloused and emotionally disconnected with my parents and extended family. I still maintained a friendly relationship with both my parents, and I always sought to honor them, but I was not terribly motivated to go out of my way to spend extended amounts of time with either of them or my siblings. Had it not been for my wife, Donna, encouraging bridge building, I don't know where my relationships with my parents might have ended up. Donna has always been very aware of the tension that has existed in my family dynamic, and, in fact, she has been hurt on occasion by various members of my family. Yet her commitment to bridge building has never waned. She has made it her mission to initiate getting together with my family, even when she knew it was uncomfortable for me, and even when the fun-factor wasn't very high for either of us. She has also done the same thing with her extended family, acting as the go-between when tensions were high and relationships were strained. God put it in Donna's heart to have a great love for family, and rather than to take the easy path of "whatever will be, will be," she has waged a tenacious fight for unity, both in her family and in mine. The result is relationships on both ends that are much stronger than they otherwise would have been had she laid down her arms when she was battle-weary.

Once again, honor must extend to in-laws, and any encouragement by a spouse to not follow this mandate is to lead one's spouse into grave sin. Jesus did not mince words when it comes to those who tempt others to sin.

> **"What sorrow awaits the world, because it tempts people to sin. Temptations are inevitable, but what sorrow awaits the person who does the tempting."**
> *-Matthew 18:7* (NLT)

The encouragement of healthy family relationships even among in-laws is hugely important, because by this the Kingdom of God is built up. It is God's will that His Kingdom be built partly through healthy families who are engaged in expressing His characteristics in the earth. And the characteristics of healthy families are forgiveness, love, unity, and loyalty through thick and thin.

Honor and Dishonor in the Church

One issue I have with many of today's churches is the trend toward dividing up the age groups into "contemporary services" and "traditional services." In other words, many churches have chosen to segregate the ages of their congregations into young and old by offering an early traditional service that features the singing of old hymns and traditional songs, and later offering a second service featuring modern, contemporary music that appeals to the younger generation. The reason I believe this is an unfortunate movement is because the church is supposed to be a family, and as families we are supposed to do important things – like worshiping God – together. How can the younger generation exercise their mandate to honor their elders in the church if the leaders segregate them into their own little groups? How can the younger generation learn from the wisdom and experience of the older generation if they never see them at church? And how can the older generation benefit from the energy, service, and forward thinking of the younger generation if the age groups are simply like two ships passing in the night and never interact in the house of God? It seems like the attitude of the younger generation in many churches is that we "we want worship to be our way, and we don't want any part of the boring old ways of our forbearers." Surprisingly, church leaders are catering to this! What's wrong with "blended worship," where old and young alike are in the same room enjoying each others' company and worshiping God together with a blend of old and new songs?

I have some questions for church leaders and the younger generation of churchgoers: How can the younger generation exercise the honor of elders if they are never even in the same room with them? And how can a person truly honor God if they are not honoring the ones God says to honor?

Honor Brings a Sure Reward

If you want to be good at life, then learn to honor and esteem elders, overseers, all those in authority, and, particularly, your parents and grandparents. And if you see ignorance and foolishness in those over you, then pray for them and do all you can to respectfully help them, and maybe they will see the light. You can't help them by dishonoring them. You only harm yourself that way. But honor brings a sure reward.

"Instead of being critical of people in authority over you and envious of their position, be happy you're not responsible for everything they have to do. Instead of piling on complaints, thank

them for what they do. Overwhelm them with encouragement and appreciation!"
-Joyce Meyer

"Our parents deserve our honor and respect for giving us life itself. Beyond this they almost always made countless sacrifices as they cared for and nurtured us through our infancy and childhood, provided us with the necessities of life, and nursed us through physical illnesses and the emotional stresses of growing up."
-Ezra Taft Benson

"Let parents bequeath to their children not riches, but the spirit of reverence."
-Plato

"Football is like life - it requires perseverance, self-denial, hard work, sacrifice, dedication and respect for authority."
-Vince Lombardi

11

"Dance with the One Who Brung Ya."

Have you ever heard that saying, "Dance with the one who brung ya?" It has the picture of a young man inviting a young lady to a dance or party, going out of his way to pick her up and paying for the evening, and then taking her to the dance only to have her dance with other men. It's a wise old saying that speaks to the importance of loyalty toward those who have invested in you.

Proverbs 19:22 alludes to this as well. It says, **"What is desirable in a man is his fidelity."** The New Living Translation renders it like this: **"Loyalty makes a person attractive."**

God values loyalty, and He honors it.

This is one of the reasons why I believe I have been blessed in business, because I have always danced with the one who brung me. I have always been loyal in the business setting. When I was still young and inexperienced, a man by the name of Jim Shaddle, the CEO and owner of a nutriceutical company, saw something in me that I didn't even see in myself. He believed in me, invested money in my educational process, and trained me according to the principles he knew would help me – and thus him – to prosper. He was also patient with my long learning curve when my knowledge was small and my presentation skills were rough and clunky.

As a result of his investment in me, I began to prosper in that business. And as I did, other people began to take notice. I was later contacted by job recruiters in the pharmaceutical industry asking me if I would consider making a career move. One of the competing companies in my niche of the field reached out to me about job openings, and I can't count the number of times doctors have approached me about working in their clinics as a consultant, or getting me involved in a marketing program. But I never expressed interest in any of these opportunities, even though some of them looked attractive. And even during some lean years when the business seemed to be going south, I still did not leap over into supposedly greener pastures for the sake of escaping my circumstances. Why? Because it was Mr. Shaddle who invested in me, not one of these other people who just wanted to benefit from Mr. Shaddle's time and expense. It was him who helped get me where I eventually went in my business, and therefore it was his company and his interests that I aligned my heart to. And God has blessed me because of that sense of loyalty.

Now, Mr. Shaddle and I have not always seen eye-to-eye. There are some things he has done and said, in fact, that have made me downright fuming mad. There are times I wished he would have done things differently. But I figure if I was smart enough to run a business like his, it would be me in that position, and not him. In spite of our differences in some areas, my loyalty to him remained steadfast until which time it was obvious that a move out would benefit both him and me equally.

You see, being a student of Proverbs since my late twenties, I read and obeyed a passage of Scripture many years ago that has benefited me in business ever since.

The one who guards a fig tree will eat its fruit,
and whoever protects their master will be honored.
–Proverbs 27:18 (NIV)

The New Living Translation renders it like this:

As workers who tend a fig tree are allowed to eat the fruit, so workers who protect their employer's interests will be rewarded.

I have always tried to live by that. I have tried to never just think of myself when it comes to my relationship with those over me. I wish I could say that was always true of the past ministry positions I was in, but I've learned along those lines, too. Loyalty to those who have invested in you to help make you what you are today is a very, very important principle to God, and it should be to us. It's a principle of honor, which God esteems highly, but which our culture now knows very little.

Even though this verse in Proverbs is speaking mostly of a business relationship between an employer and an employee, or even a master and a slave, such as was the case with loyal and faithful Joseph in Egyptian slavery, we can see this principle at work even in relationships that were not in the realm of business.

For example, do you remember when Abraham won a great military victory over an alliance of three kings and gained a huge amount of plunder? Scripture records in Genesis 14 that Abraham tithed from that plunder to the priest, Melchizedek. This is significant, so pay close attention.

Who was Melchizedek? Theories abound. Some say it was the pre-incarnate Christ. Maybe so. But a historical book of the time suggests something else. The ancient book of Jasher, which was a highly regarded historical record of the time, so highly regarded that it was referenced three times in the Bible, says that Melchizedek was Noah's son, Shem, who later became a priest in that region where Abraham lived. Jasher records that when Abraham left his father's house and set out on his own, he was taken in by Shem and lived with him for a time, and Shem taught Abraham the ways of the Lord.

So when Abraham was again out on his own with his own

family and own estate, he felt it was the loyal and honorable thing to do to give back to the man who had invested in him.

This is a theme seen all throughout scripture. Loyal and honorable people like Joseph, David, Daniel, and many others, never ran out on those who invested in them, even when staying put was not desirable. However, we do see in scripture examples of people who *did* run out, and what the outcome was.

Here are three examples:

There was a young man by the name of John Mark who was one of the Apostle Paul's ministry partners. After casting his allegiance to Paul and his ministry, John Mark set out on a missionary journey with Paul, only to abandon him and go back home when things didn't pan out to his liking. Later, John Mark changed his tune again and wanted to head out with Paul and Barnabas on another missionary journey. But Paul refused. Paul no longer trusted John Mark because he had not shown himself faithful. Paul wanted people he could depend on, not people who changed with the tides.

Another example is found in the book of Philemon. Philemon was a businessman and owned slaves, or what might be better described as household servants. He had a servant named, Onesimus, who ran away. In Paul's letter to Philemon, he did not excuse the actions of the runaway slave. Instead, he acknowledged that it was the right thing to do for Onesimus to return to Philemon. By this time Paul had become fond of Onesimus, who had become an important part of Paul's ministry. As Paul said in Philemon 1:13, *"I would have liked to keep him with me…, but I did not want to do anything without your consent."*

Now, the backstory is important to understand the significance of Paul's position in this situation.

Onesimus came into the faith as a result of Paul's ministry. Philemon, too, was Paul's son in the faith from some time earlier. Yet Paul did not demand anything from Philemon in the situation with Onesimus, because Paul understood the importance of things done honorably, and with a high degree of integrity and loyalty. So he appealed to Philemon to receive Onesimus back as now a friend and brother in Christ. But take note: Even though Onesimus had now been separated from Philemon for a long time, and even though Onesimus had now come into the faith and was now Paul's faithful ministry partner on whom he had come to rely, Paul knew it was the right thing to do for Onesimus to go back and fulfill his duty to Philemon. It was going to cost Paul an important ministry partner to send Onesimus back, but he knew it was the honorable thing for them both to do in order to represent Christ's interests in a spirit of integrity. And obviously, Onesimus consented to this, even though he knew he was likely to be placed back into the role of a slave. Honor and loyalty were upheld.

The third example on the importance of loyalty – and it is perhaps the most striking example of all – is that of Lot, Abraham's nephew. Again, the backstory is important to understand the point.

Before God changed his name, when Abraham was still known as Abram, Lot had come into Abram's clan as a young man and was now prospering alongside his uncle because of the blessing that was on Abram's life. Abram made Lot who he was. His guidance and wisdom benefited Lot greatly. And when Lot began to prosper as well, his herds and flocks became so large that the regions where they were grazing could not contain both his flocks and Abram's massive number of animals. So when the herdsmen of both men began to argue, Abram made Lot an offer.

> [8] *So Abram said to Lot, "Let's not have any quarreling between you and me, or between your herders and mine, for we are close relatives.* [9] *Is not the whole land before you? Let's part company. If you go to the left, I'll go to the right; if you go to the right, I'll go to the left."*
> -**Genesis 13:8-9** (NIV)

And how did Lot respond?

> [10] *Lot looked around and saw that the whole plain of the Jordan toward Zoar was well watered, like the garden of the Lord, like the land of Egypt. (This was before the Lord destroyed Sodom and Gomorrah.)* [11] *So Lot chose for himself the whole plain of the Jordan and set out toward the east. The two men parted company:* [12] *Abram lived in the land of Canaan, while Lot lived among the cities of the plain and pitched his tents near Sodom.* (NIV)

Pay attention. Even though Abram gave Lot the choice of land, Lot gave no honor to his uncle who had invested so much in him when he made his decision. He chose the best land for himself, and gave Abram what was left. And his uncle honored that choice. But God didn't. God honored Abram for being gracious to Lot, but what became of Lot as a result of his choice?

Scripture doesn't mention Lot again until chapter 19 of Genesis. By this time Lot and his family were living inside the city of Sodom among that wicked culture. Because of the prayers of Abram (now called, Abraham, by this time), God sent angels to remove Lot from Sodom before destroying it. But here is where we see how the consequences of Lot's decision to separate from Abraham the way he did become apparent.

Now removed from the blessing connected to Abraham, Lot's selfish pursuits catch up with him. He ends up no longer living on the plains enjoying safe pasture, but now fully within the most wicked culture of that time. While still maintaining a degree of integrity and honor of God, still, the culture had affected him and his family more than he knew. When the evil men of that city approached Lot's door demanding him to send out the "men" (angels) who were in Lot's house so they could rape them, Lot did something outrageous. In an effort to redirect attention off the angels, as if the angels couldn't take care of themselves, Lot actually offered his daughters instead to the perverse desires of the men of the town! Can you imagine?!

Well, the angels got Lot and his family out before the city was destroyed, but Lot's wife, too, had more of Sodom in her than she realized. When she looked back longingly at the burning city in direct disobedience to the command of God through the angels, God turned her into a pillar of salt.

In no time at all, Lot soon found himself hiding out in a cave with this two daughters, his fortunes gone, his home evaporated, and his wife and sons-in-law-to-be all slain. And to add insult to injury, his daughters feared they would never see civilization or humanity again because of their long isolation in that cave. In a desperate attempt to carry on their family line, both daughters decided to do something so perverse that it demonstrates how much of the wickedness of Sodom had affected them as well. On consecutive nights, Lot's daughters got their father very drunk and took turns having sexual relations with him in the hopes of conceiving and having children. And conceive they did. Can you imagine his horror when Lot finally realized what had happened? Those incestuous sons, Moab and Ben-Ammi, became the patriarchs of two very wicked cultures, the Moabites and Ammonites, who were murderous, idol-worshiping pagans.

All this came about as the ultimate result of one terrible decision on Lot's part: taking the easy way out and looking only to his own interests without considering the welfare of the one who was over him and who had invested so much in him.

There are sometimes terrible consequences to a lack of loyalty and looking out only for yourself without considering the welfare of others. In all things we must seek to obey the command of Philippians 2:4:

"Do not merely look out for your own personal interests, but also for the interests of others." (NAS)

Obedience to Philippians 2:4 should have special emphasis when it comes to the people in our lives who have invested in us. Spend a few moments right taking inventory of your life.

What are the things you enjoy today as a result of the investments others have made in you? Who are the people who have made those investments? Perhaps it is your parents. Maybe it is a distant relative or a family friend. It could be a pastor or a youth ministry leader. It could even be a teacher. If you want to be good at life, you will take time to thank God for the investment He has made in you through these people, and then you will show thankfulness, loyalty, and honor toward those who have made those investments. It's what people who are good at life do, because they know that a universal law is always at work: *whatever you sow, you will eventually reap.* When you sow loyalty and honor, loyalty and honor is what will come back to you. But when you look out only for "number one" and forget the ones who have invested in you like Lot did, the reaping process works against you.

"Jehovah had nothing to say to Moses and the others about the care of the planet. He had plenty to say about tribal loyalty and conquest."
-E. O. Wilson

"If having a soul means being able to feel love and loyalty and gratitude, then animals are better off than a lot of humans."
-James Herriot

"So much of what is best in us is bound up in our love of family, that it remains the measure of our stability because it measures our sense of loyalty. All other pacts of love or fear derive from it and are modeled upon it."
-Haniel Long

"My whole thing is loyalty. Loyalty over royalty; word is bond."
-Fetty Wap

"When people show loyalty to you, you take care of those who are with you. It's how it goes with everything. If you have a small circle of friends, and one of those friends doesn't stay loyal to you, they don't stay your friend for very long."
-John Cena

"What is a disloyal act? A person is disloyal if he treats you as a stranger when, in fact, he belongs to you as a friend or partner. Each of us is bound to some special others by the invisible fibers of loyalty."
-Lewis B. Smedes

"If you're not loyal to your team, you can get by for a while, but eventually you will need to rely on their loyalty to you, and it just won't be there."
-Tim Schafer

"I look for these qualities and characteristics in people. Honesty is number one, respect, and absolutely the third would have to be loyalty."
-Summer Altice

12

The Refiner's Fire

There once was a young man who lived the life of a fugitive, constantly on the run, hiding out in caves, and fleeing for his life from a madman who was bent on destroying him. As the years passed he began to gather around himself other displaced or disgruntled men, and eventually the group grew into a fairly large band of outlaws; although, really, they weren't outlaws at all. They weren't murderous marauders or thieves, just men who had the common goal of survival, and there was strength and safety in numbers.

Their leader's name was David, a young man who had been anointed the next king of Israel. Yet he could not assume his throne until his eventual predecessor, King Saul, was dead, but it was this same King Saul who was the madman who would at times mobilize large portions of his army just to hunt David. Saul's jealousy of David had morphed him into a monster.

Since David had already been anointed as the next king, no one in that time and place would have faulted him or held him guilty for hastening the process by killing a crazed king who had literally become so demon possessed that he once killed 70 different priests and their entire families simply because they had helped David as he fled for his life. In fact, on two occasions God put Saul into David's hands. But even at the insistent urging of his men to end Saul when those opportunities came, David would not do it, stating that he would "not touch the Lord's anointed."

What an honorable heart David had! What character! What nobility! Rather than taking the road of instant relief by taking matters into his own hands even as he was leading the terrible life of a fugitive, David waited on God, even though circumstances indicated that it was God Himself Who arranged for Saul to fall into David's hands. And yes, it was indeed God Who arranged that. But it was not for the purpose of ending Saul at the hands of David. It was not for the purpose of ending David's undesirable circumstances immediately. Rather, it was for the purpose of testing David's heart.

Let me say that another way.

When circumstances indicated that God had placed David in a situation that required him to act, things were not as they seemed. God wasn't leading David to kill Saul at all, even though all the people around David were counseling him on what they interpreted as the will of God. Rather, those two occasions where killing Saul seemed like the most reasonable thing to do, *David was being tested!* Against the imploring of his men who were also leading the lives of fugitives, David refused to give into their urging. Why? Because David knew about what was honorable. And he knew that instant gratification leads to consequences, while delayed gratification for the sake of doing the honorable thing leads to reward.

And, boy, did David ever pass that test! As a result, David went down in history as the most respected and the most beloved King ever in Israel's history, "a man after God's own heart." God indeed took care of both Saul and David according to what they deserved in *His* time, and the outcome was better than what David could have produced himself.

So then, let's apply that lesson to the situation in which you now find yourself. Perhaps it's undesirable. Maybe the arrival of that which you have been dreaming seems delayed, and it is tempting to take matters into your own hands and act, much like Abraham and Sarah did when they tried to fulfill the promise of a child their own way, resulting in a terrible mess. Maybe you're chomping at the bit to move forward, and there seems to be a logical and "spiritual" way out. But what if you're being tested? What if there is a reward up ahead that God wants to lavish on you, and a calling He wants to eventually bring you into, but He has to chisel your character before you can get there? What if the discomfort you are in is exactly where God wants you right now? This is why it says in James 1:2-4,

> **Consider pure joy, my brethren, when you encounter various trials, knowing that the testing of your faith produces patience. And let patience have her perfect work, that you may be mature and complete, not lacking anything.** (NAS)

Did you catch that? The *testing of your faith! Various trials! Patience!* It all works together. You can't get to the *"not lacking anything"* part without the patience. And you can't get to the patience part without having to exercise it in the midst of various trials that vex you.

I'm convinced that God will orchestrate certain situations in believers' lives where they are forced to exercise patience, and I now believe that this is one of the reasons why He ordained the church, because the church is the very place where the virtues of patience, perseverance, and selfless service are exercised. The church is one of the best places where Christians are tested, and when people pass the tests and persevere through various trials, God then has a legal right to bless certain people more than others! No one can ever accuse God of unfairly lavishing blessing on some people more than others, because the tests that certain people pass give Him that right that no one can challenge.

Sometimes God wants people to stay in certain situations even though it is uncomfortable for them because He has something He wants to teach them, some character He wants them to develop, and some flesh He wants to kill! But when they bail out and abort that process for the sake of their comfort or convenience, they have to go around the same mountain again somewhere else. You see, when people bail out on God's chiseling process, they will get relief momentarily and all will seem great for a little while because they are out from under the heat of the refining fire. But then they find that after some time they are right back in the heat of the fire again. "Out of the frying pan, into the fire," as the saying goes. They don't understand why they go around the same mountains over and over again and can't seem to make significant progress. It's because they are trail jumpers. God has them on one trail, and as soon as it gets rocky they jump the trail. Then God lovingly leads them through other methods, eventually getting them back onto a similar path, and as soon as they hit that rocky patch again, they find "spiritual" reasons to once again jump the trail. And around and around the mountain they go!

Some people never do learn to submit to God's chastening process. As soon as things get uncomfortable or go differently than they think it should, they pull up roots again and relocate, and they forfeit the growth and blessing process that God has in mind. This is true of people in marriages, in careers, and in churches. People who persevere through difficulty in marriages are usually stronger as a result. People who persevere through trials in their career will usually learn from those experiences and climb the corporate ladder and gain the benefits of seniority. And people who learn to voluntarily submit themselves to the Potter's shaping process in their church will grow in maturity, in wisdom, and in ministry fruitfulness.

"But what about what is 'best' for me and my family," a person might ask.

Listen, as difficult as this might be to understand, and as much as it violates our Americanized version of *me-centered* Christianity, life in Christ is not just about what is immediately beneficial to you and your family. We must always consider how God's Kingdom works, and God always has in mind your long-term benefit. Your long-term benefit, however, will often mean you will need to sacrifice short term comfort.

In doing so, the acid test question must always be asked: "How will this decision affect others?" We must always consider how our actions will affect someone else, and how it affects God's church according to the command of Philippians 2:4: **"Look not just to your own interests, but also to the interests of OTHERS."**

It reminds me of now-famous pastor, Keith Moore, who used to work under the late Kenneth Hagin and his ministry. About ten years into Keith's service to Pastor Hagin, he felt God was calling him into his own ministry. Yet he did not go right out and leave Pastor Hagin high and dry and launch his own ministry. He waited for the proper timing. In fact, he waited, and waited and waited until God put everything in order. He waited for another ten years! And when he did launch out on his own, it was like God shot him out of a cannon! His ministry catapulted nearly overnight to international status and influence. Keith Moore did things right, in the right time, and with a high degree of honor, thinking not just of himself, but also the interests of others. And God greatly rewarded him for it.

What if God is Testing You?

Today's shallow, me-centered culture has very little tolerance for discomfort. Instant gratification rules our society, and the younger the person, the more pronounced this tendency seem to be. Practically gone are the days when people understood and practiced delayed gratification for future reward. I heard pastor Keith Moore once say that while our society preaches "get it now any how," God's methods are, "if you'll wait, it'll be great."

Unfortunately, the church in America leans toward the instant gratification camp over the delayed gratification camp. "My way or the highway" seems to rule the day. But if you want to be blessed beyond measure, God says in so many words, "It's MY way, not your way."

God's people in America today largely do not understand that one of God's methods in refining His people and chiseling their character is often placing them in situations that are uncomfortable or undesirable in some way, requiring them to be diligent, trustworthy, and honorable even in situations where they would like nothing better than to escape.

I know many people who are both knowledgeable in the Word and tremendously talented, but have never learned to put down roots anywhere and submit to God's refining process. They lend their talents to churches for a time, for example, only to jump ship abruptly and move on to another church after a couple of years or so, starting the process all over again, claiming, of course, that God was leading them. Some have burned bridges with so many churches that they end up not attending church at all eventually, and instead of using their talents for Kingdom purposes, they end up using them for less noble pursuits. Well-meaning and sincere though they might be, they never learn to submit to God's chastening and discipline, and therefore the call that is on their lives flounder and fall silent.

It's very sad that people forfeit what God has called them to through unfaithfulness. God gives them that choice. He gives you and I the same choice, and He honors whatever choice we make, even if the choice will cause us harm eventually. We can do things our own way and reject the temporary discomfort associated with the refining process, claiming that it is God's leading, and eventually pay a high price in the end. Or, we can submit to God's chastening process and delay our gratification, and receive a reward after we have been found faithful.

A key concept here is that the very definition of faithfulness is sticking to something when your mind and flesh are screaming to do something else. Faithfulness by nature means looking past temporary discomfort for the sake of future reward, as Jesus did when for the joy set before Him (future reward) He scorned the shame of the cross (see Hebrews 12:1-2).

It was Jesus, in fact, who told the parable of the talents (see

Matthew 25:14-30), demonstrating the rewards of faithfulness with another person's interests and property, and the consequences of unfaithfulness. Jesus also once said,

> *"One who is faithful in a very little is also faithful in much... And if you have not been faithful in that which is another's, who will give you that which is your own?*
> -**Luke 16:10,12** (ESV)

You have to show faithfulness and good stewardship with another person's business or ministry before God will entrust you with more. We can either do things right with the benefit of God's church and His leaders in mind, and, in turn, reap the rewards of doing things honorably, or we can think only of ourselves, our families, and our ministries, and then later reap the consequences of things done dishonorably. It's our choice. We have free will. God allows us to choose. But blessings or curses hang in the balance. As God has said,

> *This day I [God] call the heavens and the earth as witnesses against you that I have set before you life and death, blessings and curses. Now choose life, so that you and your children may live and that you may love the Lord your God, listen to His voice, and hold fast to Him.*
> –**Deuteronomy 30:19** (NIV)

It's like God was giving the ancient Israelites the answer to the test in advance. It's almost as if He was saying, "Ok, look. I'm giving you a choice here: blessings or curses. I'll lay it out for you. Blessings are good, and curses are bad. Therefore, let Me tell you what to choose. Choose the blessings! Choose life! Choose My way!" And that's what He is saying to you and me today. Choose

His way! Choose life! Choose blessings! It might not be easy in the beginning, but it will be worth it in the end.

Receiving Your Full Reward

The Bible indicates that there are different levels of reward in God's Kingdom. There are partial rewards for service, full rewards, and no rewards. This reward system has nothing to do with salvation itself, but the redeemed will receive rewards both in this life and in the one to come. The Apostle John further points out that we can lose some or all of our reward that is being stored up for us in eternity.

> *Watch out that you do not lose what we have worked so hard to achieve. Be diligent so that you receive your full reward.*
> -**2 John 8** (NLT)

Remember this and remember it well if you want to walk in God's best: **You can bail out on what God is trying to do in your life and have only the memories of the pain you** *partially* **endured, with nothing or little to show for all the time you already invested!** *Those who quit only have the testimony of quitters. But only those who persevere a long time through trial and don't quit have the testimony of a winner. Only those who have overcome something difficult can rightfully be called overcomers!* You can choose to trust God and wait it out patiently for the fulfillment of His plan to unfold in *His* time, serving with excellence and perseverance wherever God has you planted now, and eventually reap a *full* reward that will last for eternity. So many people are looking for God to zap them into their breakthrough or magically refine their character without any painful refining process. Folks, for every one time that God zaps someone out of bad character or into a breakthrough of some sort, there are 100 others who God shapes as a potter carefully shapes clay: *through time and* *pressure.* There's no way around it. This is the way it works. A muscle can't grow without resistance. And neither can a Christian.

It's yours to decide. Do you want to do things *your* way, or God's way?

"...the proof of your faith, being more precious than gold which is perishable, even though tested by fire, may be found to result in praise and glory and honor at the revelation of Jesus Christ..."
-1 Peter 1:7 (NAS)

"God desires to change us from the inside out – renewing our minds, starving our self-destructive tendencies and teaching us to form new habits."
-Beth Moore

"Those who have walked through the fire leave sparks of light everywhere they go."
-Unknown

"Great works are performed not by strength but by perseverance."
-Samuel Johnson

"Permanence, perseverance and persistence in spite of all obstacles, discouragements, and impossibilities: It is this, that in all things distinguishes the strong soul from the weak."
-Thomas Carlyle

"Perseverance is the hard work you do after you get tired of doing the hard work you already did."
-Newt Gingrich

"I do not think that there is any other quality so essential to success of any kind as the quality of perseverance. It overcomes almost everything, even nature."

-John D. Rockefeller

13

Life Lessons from an Auctioneer and a Step Father

One of the most valuable lessons I ever learned as a teenager happened when I carelessly backed my '72 Chevy Nova into my stepfather's new car and caved in the driver's door. To my surprise, he didn't freak out, and he didn't even get angry. He knew I was already upset with myself. I was more important to him than his new car. So he spared my feelings and comforted me rather than being angry. He held people and possessions in their proper order. Because of his example I was able to pass that same graciousness on to my wife many years later when she did the same thing to my new car.

One of the worst mistakes people make is exalting possessions or money over people. Part of our very existence is other people; to serve them as Christ has served us. People will most likely be around long after that possession we hold so dear has rusted or busted.

This lesson is magnified in the experience of Leslie Hindman, who served as the president of the Midwest's leading auction firm. Each year she helped to auction off millions of dollars worth of fine art and high end home furnishings from the estates of the wealthy. While her firm handled goods that are considered rare and precious by most of society, her work helped her to see what is truly important.

"I see people fighting about their stuff all the time," she said. "You realize life is not about possessions."

One such episode occurred when she was hired to hold an auction in the modest home of a suburban family whose mother had recently passed away. As Hindman led the auction, the siblings bid against each other for their mother's humble belongings, barely uttering a word to one another.

It's important to remember to always treat possessions and money as what they are: *tools that have no eternal value.* I am not suggesting that we place no value on money and possessions, because taking care of one's possessions and managing money well is also an important life principle. But don't ever let possessions occupy a place in your heart above people, and certainly not God. Use your possessions to serve people and God, be lavish in your generosity, eager to share, and inclined to give of yourself and your possessions. In doing so, you will endear yourself to people, and naturally feel better about yourself and happier with life.

This is the lesson taught by the classic story, A Christmas Carol, by Charles Dickens, in which Ebenezer Scrooge's relentless and selfish pursuit of monetary gain left him destitute in his soul and ultimately friendless in life. His ghostly epiphany taught him that happiness cannot be found in possessions, but in giving of one's self to benefit others. It was only in the act of sharing generously that Ebenezer Scrooge found the joy that had eluded him all his life.

While the story of Ebenezer Scrooge is fictional, of course, it does represent an important true-life principle: All the riches and possessions in the world cannot fill the void in one's heart that is reserved for the satisfaction and fulfillment of reaching out to others and being a blessing to mankind with whatever you find in your hands to share.

Although the moral of A Christmas Carol has been told and retold in many ways and in various art forms for generations, its message and application has strangely eluded the masses. I believe that most people probably believe in theory that family, friends, and people in general are more important the monetary things. Yet in application, money still holds a mysterious power over people that defies logic in many cases.

One example is a couple I know who had been married to one another for most of their lives and were now in their sixties. The husband was a successful businessman who owned horses and operated a chiropractic clinic. One day he suffered a brain aneurism and lapsed into a coma. As he lay unconscious, his wife leaped into action. She searched for and hired a neurologist who was willing to declare her husband a vegetable, stating that he would not survive the coma. With this information in hand, she was able to secure the rights to all her husband's assets; his bank accounts, his businesses, everything. While he lay helpless and unaware of what was happening to him, she divorced him and confiscated everything he owned. And then...he woke up. He made a full recovery, only to realize that he had awakened to a horrible nightmare worse than one he could have dreamed in his sleep. His now ex-wife had taken everything and left him completely penniless and without the means to even start over. At the time of this writing he describes the sum total of his possessions as a chair and a bed. But worse than that, his ex-wife was even able to turn his adult children against him.

There are two lessons to learn from this true story.

First, if money is not held in its proper place, it can turn once-loving people into horrible monsters who will stop at nothing to get more of it.

Secondly, people find out how truly meaningless possessions are if they cannot enjoy them with their family members by their side. While the man in this terrible situation was certainly devastated by the loss of everything he owned, his most significant loss was that of his family. Perhaps if he had spent less time pursuing money and more time investing in his family, he may have made less money, but he may have awakened from his coma with loving and concerned family members by his side and a business and home intact.

I'll close this chapter by saying that I do not share the opinion of some who claim that money has no importance. It certainly does. Money is a necessity of life, and when you have a surplus of it you can live with less stress and help more people. I'm all for doing whatever good and honest work you can to make a fruitful living for yourself and your family. However, when the pursuit of money and possessions takes such precedence that it becomes a god and crowds out the other loves in one's life, then with each dollar gained a stone is laid in the path to destruction.

Life is about balance. Sometimes people teeter back and forth over the years in trying to achieve that balance, but the wise do eventually discover what is most important in life. And hardly anyone reaches the end of their lives stretched out on their death beds wishing they had worked longer hours and made more money. What they wish is that they had invested more time in their families and in the good of humanity. But if you live with the end in mind and cherish the loved ones now with whom God has blessed you, and invest in people and in the good of mankind in whatever small or large ways you can, then at the end of your life you will look back over the landscape of your years with no regrets, and proclaim as the Apostle Paul did just before his execution,

> *"6...the time for my departure is near. 7I have fought the good fight, I have finished the race, I have kept the faith. 8Now there is in store for me the crown of righteousness, which the Lord, the righteous Judge, will award to me on that day—and not only to me, but also to all who have longed for His appearing.*
> *-2 Timothy 4:6-8* (NIV)

"Then he said to them, 'Watch out! Be on your guard against all kinds of greed; life does not consist in an abundance of possessions'."
-**Luke 12:15** (NIV)

"I showed you that by this kind of hard work we must help the weak, remembering the words the Lord Jesus himself said: 'It is more blessed to give than to receive.' "
-**Acts 20:35** (NIV)

"Give, and you will receive. Your gift will return to you in full--pressed down, shaken together to make room for more, running over, and poured into your lap. The amount you give will determine the amount you get back."
-**Luke 6:38** (NLT)

"It's good to be blessed. It's better to be a blessing."
-**Unknown**

"When I chased after money, I never had enough. When I got my life on purpose and focused on giving of myself and everything that arrived into my life, then I was prosperous."
-**Wayne Dyer**

14

This Always Profits You in the End

Our society's understanding of the term, *integrity*, is little more than simply being honest. Honesty is indeed a very important part of integrity. In fact, the worth of honesty cannot be overstated. While honesty is perhaps the bigger part of the meaning of integrity, it's not the sum of it, however.

One dictionary definition of integrity is *the quality of being honest and having strong moral principles; moral uprightness.* But again, what does it mean to be morally upright?

Perhaps to better understand integrity we should examine what it is not.

Integrity is not the same as expediency. In other words, integrity is not always convenient or pragmatic. Sometimes integrity, in fact, can be quite inconvenient and impractical. Expediency in its larger definition has to do with pursuing whatever is immediately profitable or personally advantageous or desirable without consideration of morality, principle, or ethics. Conversely, a person who is pursuing integrity – one who is highly principled – is one who embraces a high code of values and consistently lives by them, even if sticking by those values is sometimes costly.

Benjamin Disraeli, one of the more celebrated Prime Ministers of the United Kingdom from the 1800s, once said, "Principle is my motto, not expediency." It was Disraeli's high code of values that made him a great leader.

A person of integrity is not just honest, but he or she also refuses to cut corners and compromise in order to get quick results, immediate gratification, or a higher profit margin. It is true that there are many people in our world who do just that and seem to profit from it, at least initially, until their duplicity inevitably catches up with them. Life and experience teaches a bigger truth, however: **while integrity may not always profit you in the beginning, it always profits you in the end.**

I have taught my children and my church that life lived the world's way is a mirror opposite of life lived God's way. The world teaches us to live life for instant gratification and quick results no matter what it takes. But the way of the Maker of life teaches a different path. God teaches the way of principles. And the way of principles is not always gratifying, pleasing, or profitable in the beginning, but it *always* is in the end. It is only people who are highly principled who stand the test of time in business, ministry, and life in general.

Expediency is somewhat related to our understanding of *pragmatic*. Pragmatism involves a very practical approach to life. "Whatever works to get the job done quickly and inexpensively" is the motto of the pragmatic person. Pragmatism is results oriented. And while pragmatism is certainly not wrong in and of itself, without a strong code of morals to complement it, it nevertheless falls short of the high mark of integrity. Pragmatism without integrity can lead only to lower levels of thinking and behaving, such as believing that it's okay to color the truth if it helps you to achieve your goals or stay out of trouble.

Pragmatism has even found its way into the modern church. Scores of churches and pastors seem to operate with the mindset that it's okay to not preach the whole counsel of God and/or to borrow methods from the world if it makes the church more popular and draws bigger crowds. Countless pastors have deluded themselves into believing that watering down the gospel to make it more palatable and avoiding certain subjects is okay as long as more people are drawn into the church. They believe the tragically wrong ideology that the end justifies the means, failing to acknowledge that godliness and the true unadulterated gospel of Jesus Christ are incompatible with that ideology.

Once a person starts down a path of compromise, he or she slowly becomes more hardened and insensitive to the truth and will ultimately begin to justify all sorts of behaviors, eventually even rationalizing behaviors previously considered reprehensible. In studying the lives of the heroes of church history, we find a common thread in all of them: They consciously identified their values, could articulate them well, and stuck by them even if it cost them greatly. I have found personal enrichment, in fact, in reading some of the quotes from Jonathan Edwards, a Puritan preacher and philosopher of early America. It was Edwards who wrote a list of personal resolutions, which included this one: "Resolved, never to give over, nor in the least to slacken my fight with my corruptions, however unsuccessful I may be."

You see, a person of integrity is not perfect. None of us are, of course. But a person of integrity recognizes his or her corruptions and goes to war with them, winning some battles and losing others. Yet in spite of even repeated failures, he or she does not give up. He or she continues to wage war against the "sins that so easily beset us," to quote the writer of Hebrews.

Because we all have sins in our personalities that can easily beset us, and because we live in a world where indulging those besetting sins is a very easy and even celebrated road to take, we would do well to copy the heroes of the faith and know well what we believe, know why we believe it, know what is compatible and incompatible with those beliefs, and be able to articulate them, perhaps even putting certain standards in writing.

This is what the famous evangelist, Billy Graham, and his associates did. In 1948, shortly before Billy Graham became a household name, the young evangelist met with his associates in order to forge a plan for leading their ministry with integrity and avoid scandal. While it may be more the exception than the rule, the gospel has nevertheless been marred by the scandalous behavior of some ministers down through the ages, and Billy Graham and his team were determined to avoid this. Graham and his team identified four areas of concern in a written document that later became known as the Modesto Manifesto, and resolved in writing to conduct themselves with the utmost integrity. There were four areas in particular in which they felt that failure would be especially damaging. They were:

- The shady management of money
- Sexual immorality
- Badmouthing others in the ministry
- Exaggerating their accomplishments

The rest, as they say, is history. Graham and his team went on to international prominence and became the most well-known and celebrated ministry of modern times. And they didn't do it with flash. They didn't do it by watering down the gospel. They didn't do it with borrowing methods from the world. They did it simply with a commitment to integrity, and God did the rest.

Following is a list of decisions that other principled people and leaders have made:

- To be an authentic person, avoiding putting on a front or façade.
- To never exploit or take advantage of anyone, especially those who are weak, uneducated, or otherwise vulnerable.
- To be the best possible example of Christlikeness in public and private.
- To never attempt to make one's self look good by demeaning others.

- To treat all people with respect and dignity, and to never do or say anything that might bring harm or embarrassment to anyone.
- To be a good steward of one's finances, body, mind, and talents.
- If a wrong is done, to make efforts to make it right.
- To be completely faithful to one's spouse, and to maintain moral purity in body and mind.
- To never lie or shade the truth, but to be honest in all of one's dealings.

This list might represent the larger definition of integrity. Again, while honesty does indeed make up a large part of what it means to be moral, the complete definition involves much more.

I will end this chapter by reiterating that integrity – the highest level of it – is the road less traveled, and it is less traveled because integrity does not always appear to be immediately advantageous. But integrity represents a life of short term sacrifices for long term reward. That is a concept that truly successful people understand, embrace, and practice. There's no getting around the fact that integrity is an integral part of any type of success.

"I always take pains to have a clear conscience toward both God and man."
-The Apostle Paul, Acts 24:16 (ESV)

"Daniel purposed in his heart that he would not defile himself..."
-Daniel 1:8 (NIV)

"In matters of style, swim with the current. In matters of principle, stand like a rock."
-Thomas Jefferson

"The supreme quality for leadership is unquestionably integrity. Without it, no real success is possible, no matter whether it is on a section gang, a football field, in an army, or in an office."
  -Dwight D. Eisenhower

"Somebody once said that in looking for people to hire, you look for three qualities: integrity, intelligence, and energy. And if you don't have the first, the other two will kill you."
  -Warren Buffett

"Never do anything that you can't admit doing, because if you are that ashamed of whatever it is, it's probably wrong."
  -Ashly Lorenzana

"Integrity does not happen by accident. Godly character is established deliberately and intentionally."
  -Tony Cooke

15

What You can Learn from Rubberneckers and News Anchors

When you have been driving on the highway and suddenly run into a random traffic jam, you probably reason to yourself that there is an accident blocking the lanes up ahead. As you keep inching ahead for what seems like forever, you finally get to where the bottleneck occurred and you notice that it is indeed an accident, but you also observe that every crashed car, every police officer, ambulance or any other type of emergency vehicle or potential traffic hindrance is completely off to the side of the road, not even affecting any of the lanes! The accident could even be on the other side of the road, yet there was bumper-to-bumper traffic for blocks or even miles! Why? *Rubberneckers!* Curious people inevitably slow down to a snail's pace just so they can stare at the wreckage on the side of the road, thus causing major traffic jams. While this is very frustrating for anyone to learn that they just sat in traffic for 30 minutes simply because people felt the need to slow down and gawk, be honest with yourself for a moment. What do you do when you finally drive up to the scene of the accident? Don't lie. We look, don't we?! We almost can't help ourselves *not* to look! Yet on the occasions that there may be an awe-inspiring sunset splashing the sky with blazing colors, or a glorious mountain view breaking the horizon, traffic speeds along unimpeded as if people don't notice or care.

There's only one explanation for why traffic bottles up because of an accident that isn't even blocking the road, but the glories of nature seem too trivial to notice. It's because **we are more attracted to the shocking, horrible, destructive and scandalous.** It's in our fallen nature to stare shamelessly when we pass an accident on the side of the road, because our minds are geared for survival, not necessarily to make us happy. At its simplest and most basic function, the default position of the mind is to simply keep us alive, so it's always on guard and on the lookout for the threatening or destructive. The media and Hollywood understand this, of course, and that's why the news, television programs, and radio are filled with awful, outrageous and appalling stories.

I have a friend whose wife is a television news anchor. One night while we were all dining out I got bold and asked her why the news focuses mostly on bad news. I appreciated her honest reply. She said, "We have a saying in our industry that goes like this: 'Good news is *no* news, and bad news is good news.'" In other words, she was explaining what a lot people already know if they are paying attention, and that's that bad news is good news for the news channels because they can sensationalize bad news and make it sell, whereas good news can't be sensationalized and therefore doesn't sell as well. Like the traffic jam example, people tend to gravitate to the sensational, even if we know that what we are watching is "spun" by the networks to be sensationalized.

On a side note, remember that news channels are simply businesses, and they are selling a product. They are not public services, for the most part, but are forms of entertainment – and even propaganda – selling a worldview and peddling junk food for the mind.

Since it's so easy for our minds to gravitate toward the negative and sinful, and since there is so much negative input readily available and pushed into our faces, we must therefore make a conscious and proactive effort to constantly feed our minds with positive, healthy, and inspiring input. This is why Philippians 4:8 instructs us to think and dwell on things that are *"true, whatever is noble, whatever is right, whatever is pure, whatever is lovely, whatever is admirable,"* things that are *"excellent or praiseworthy."* If we do this, we can rise above the masses who tend to crave mental junk food.

Albert Einstein said, *"If you feed your mind as often as you feed your stomach, then you'll never have to worry about feeding your stomach or a roof over your head or clothes on your back."*

Medical science and the field of psychology have proven that what a person constantly thinks about can largely determine one's course in life. This is also a principle taught by success materials across the world: **You become what you think about most of the time.**

Thoughts, though, are determined largely by what one puts into one's mind. What a person chooses to read, listen to, and watch on a regular basis will affect the way a person thinks. There's no way it can't, because that's how the mind, body, and spirit work. Your physical, mental, emotional, spiritual, and even financial health is a result of what you feed on.

Think of the mind as a computer program, and one's life as the computer itself. Just as a computer can only do what it has been programmed to do, a person's life can only operate according to the "programming" of the information fed into it.

The happiest and most successful people I know are those who are choosey about what they put into their minds. This is even true, to some degree, of non-religious people. Even the non-religious people I know who live relatively happy and successful lives are those who are selective and scrutinizing about what they expose their minds to. The most successful and intelligent people tend to be the ones who gravitate toward the more enriching materials and entertainment – the things that the rest of the world might consider "snooty" or "boring" – while others gravitate toward things that will simply stimulate their emotions and/or base appetites but not their intellect.

As an example, it has been said that leaders are readers. But leaders don't read just anything. Leaders don't feed their minds on pop culture magazines and novels. They read self-development books and materials that help to make them better people in as many areas as possible. Additionally, they are very choosy about their entertainment choices, choosing to entertain themselves less than the average person and develop themselves more. In fact, *Body for Life* author, Bill Phillips, who made his fortune as a nationally known fitness coach, once said, "TV is the biggest time waster in the world!"

I once heard a success guru lecturing on this very topic, and he said that most Americans' entertainment versus enrichment ratio is probably about 50 to 1. In other words, most people entertain themselves about 50 times more than they enrich themselves. This lecturer said that if people would just cut that ratio in half, choosing to entertain themselves a little less and, instead, do something that feeds their minds and enriches their intellects and spirits a little more, then they would be so far ahead of the curve of the average person that no one would ever catch them again. But alas, average people are average because they do what average people do. It's only the minority that invests in themselves as a matter of lifestyle.

The most successful people, for the most part, tend to be ones who care more about personal development than constantly entertaining themselves. When they do entertain themselves, they are choosy about what they let into their minds, because they know a truth articulated in Proverbs, that what a person allows into their hearts and minds will eventually affect their lives in some form.

As has been aptly said, *Observe what successful people do and do those same things.* The opposite would also be true: *Observe what unsuccessful people do, and avoid doing those same things.* Intelligent and successful people feed on intelligent things, while unintelligent people feed on unintelligent things, and both groups in turn tend to lead lives in keeping with what they feed on and think about.

"Above all else, guard your heart, for everything you do flows from it."
-Proverbs 4:23 (NIV)

"A wise person is hungry for knowledge, while the fool feeds on trash."
-Proverbs 15:14 (NLT)

"For as a man thinketh in his heart, so is he."
-Proverbs 23:7 (KJV)

"You are what you think. All that you are arises from your thoughts. With your thoughts you make your world."
-Anonymous

16

People Don't Care How Much You Know…

A saying I learned many years ago has been one I have tried to remember, although not always perfectly, in the way I conduct my relationships: *"People don't care how much you know until they know how much you care."*

That is so true!

Although I have known this saying for many years and tried to apply it in business and relationships, I was exposed to this truth yet again recently when I read an article about pastoral care. The author of the article, himself a pastor, explained that he went through a time in his ministry when he, like many pastors, spent more time constructing and refining his sermons than he did on his relational skills. As a result, his well-studied sermons were met with criticism. He initially responded by studying more and working on his delivery, etc. But the criticisms seemed to increase. He eventually learned through years of experience that as he reached out to people and got involved in their lives and they became his friends, people began to respond very favorably to his messages, even though nothing had changed in how he was crafting his sermons. What is true in every facet of life, then, is also true in ministry, that it is nearly impossible to inspire and compel people if they don't sense that you genuinely care about them and they are important to you.

Most people, other than your mother and father, could not care less how talented you are, how intelligent you are, how much money you make, what kind of car you drive, etc., until they know how much you care about them. In fact, a person with high intelligence, unusual talent and savvy business prowess will invite only ridicule and derision if they don't know how to make other people feel important and liked. People will even sometimes despise your talent and even your humor if you don't know how to make them feel like a million bucks.

The sooner you understand that other people don't think about you that much because they are too busy thinking about themselves, the sooner you will master relationships, business, and ministry. As stated already in chapter one, whatever talent, intelligence, or resources with which you have been blessed, understand that they were given for the express purpose of serving others, not yourself. In fact, I have become convinced that some of the people that God has blessed with unusual talent and knowledge are some of the same ones that He cannot use or bless in any significant way because they are so busy showing off and promoting themselves. When God says that He gives grace to the humble but resists the proud, that's exactly what He means. He literally resists people – even Christian people – who are full of themselves and who use their God-given abilities to simply promote themselves. The opposite is also true. People with only a moderate amount of talent and intelligence can be greatly used and blessed by God because they position themselves for promotion through their humility.

In your interactions with others, then, downplay your own talents, accomplishments, and knowledge. Don't draw attention to yourself. If someone happens to notice your skills or knowledge and comments on them, be gracious, of course, and thank them. But then deflect the compliment, if possible, and shine the spotlight back on them, something like this: "Oh, thank you. That's very nice of you to say. But I must say, I'm very impressed with your...," and then compliment that person on something you genuinely admire.

Some people can't wait for an opportunity to be the center of attention with their humor, knowledge, or talent. But don't ever use your humor at the expense of someone else, and don't ever insert your knowledge into a conversation just to show off how much you know. Your knowledge should always be offered as a way to truly benefit people in some way, but even then it must be offered humbly. Here's a suggestion in offering your knowledge without looking like a know-it-all. "You know, I might be wrong – I often am – but I read something the other day that might be helpful here." But at other times it might be the best thing to simply be silent and let other people shine.

"If you show off do not get upset when God doesn't show up."
-Matshona Dhliwayo

"When there are many words, sin is unavoidable, but the one who controls his lips is wise."
-Proverbs 10:19 (NAS)

"The wise don't make a show of their knowledge, but fools broadcast their foolishness."
-Proverbs 12:23 (NLT)

"All of you, clothe yourselves with humility toward one another, because, "God opposes the proud but shows favor to the humble."
-1 Peter 5:5 (NIV)

"Perhaps the less we have, the more we are required to brag."
-John Steinbeck

17

Counseling in the Barber's Chair

"I don't know why I'm telling you all this. It's like you're my counselor." These were the words of a complete stranger, the man who was cutting my hair for the first time.

I used to be one of those people who found it more comfortable to sit quietly in the barber's chair and not speak until spoken to. But then I found that some barbers are as shy as I used to be. So I have trained myself to ask people questions about themselves and draw them out. Well, this particular barber didn't need any drawing out; he was already good at talking. But by this time I was already in the habit of initiating conversations by asking questions, so I began asking about his family. As the barber began to tell me about his family, a volley began. He would return my "serves" by answering my questions, and I returned his volleys by asking more questions. Before very long this man was telling me about his son with whom he had a lot of relational problems. It was like a dam broke as the man just opened up. He began asking my advice, and I offered a few suggestions. But I mostly just listened and expressed interest. And that was probably like a cool drink of water to someone dying of thirst. Most people are so eager to talk about themselves that when they appear to "listen," all they are doing is waiting for their turn. So when a person finds someone who seems genuinely eager to listen with interest, they latch on!

Try it sometime. This week make a point to ask someone about his or her job, favorite hobby, or children, and then just sit back and watch how they come alive and warm up to you. You might spend the next hour talking, and actually, you won't have to do much of it. You might simply ask a few more questions and make a few affirming comments. The other party may do 90% of the talking once you get him or her going, but he or she will likely come away from the conversation thinking of you as a very enriching person and a great conversationalist.

One thing I know about myself is that I am not a witty conversationalist who is the life of the party or the center of attention at dinner gatherings. Yet many people have nevertheless told me that they find me enjoyable to speak with, and it's mostly because I am by nature a good listener. I sometimes wish that I was a more interesting person and had a lively sense of humor. Rather than trying to be something I'm not, however, I decided long ago to develop the one skill I already had, which is listening to people. Developing that one skill has won me many friends and loyal business clients. An added benefit about the fine art of listening is that it's not difficult at all. The only things you have to remember are,

1) People are not as interested in you as they are themselves, so forget your need to talk about yourself.
2) Be genuinely interested in others, because there just might be something you learn from them or there just might be something you might be able to help them with.
3) Ask questions and keep asking them.
4) You have two ears and one mouth, so listen twice as much as you talk. When you can master this, you can master people, and they will love you.

One last point about the fine art of listening. M. Scott Peck said, *"You cannot truly listen to anyone and do anything else at the same time."* Our society has become very inconsiderate along these lines. Smart phones have become the bane of human interaction. Smart phones are wonderful tools in some respects, but they are also strangely addicting to many people, to the point that a growing number of people would rather look at a smart phone during a conversation than to look a real person in the eyes and show interest in what others have to say. Please take note of this very important truth: *you listen as much with your eyes as you do with your ears.* Learn to look people in the eyes and show genuine interest in them as you let them talk. As you do, you will become known as a very engaging person, even if you don't have much to say.

> *"Guard your steps when you go to the house of God. Go near to listen rather than to offer the sacrifice of fools, who do not know that they do wrong. Do not be quick with your mouth, do not be hasty in your heart to utter anything before God. God is in heaven and you are on earth, so let your words be few. ...many words mark the speech of a fool. ... Just as there is futility in many dreams, so also in many words. Therefore, fear God!"*
> *-Ecclesiastes 5:1-3, 7* (NIV)

> *"Wisdom is the reward you get for a lifetime of listening when you'd have preferred to talk."*
> *-Doug Larson*

> *"Most of the successful people I've known are the ones who do more listening than talking."*
> *-Bernard Baruch*

"Most people do not listen with the intent to understand; they listen with the intent to reply."
-Stephen R. Covey

"Listening is a magnetic and strange thing, a creative force. The friends who listen to us are the ones we move toward. When we are listened to, it creates us, makes us unfold and expand."
-Karl A. Menninger

18

Guilty by Association

I heard about a young man who lived not too far away who happened to be hanging out with some friends one night, and those friends decided to rob a store. They ended up shooting and killing someone in the process, and although this teenager was only in the car and not participating in the dirty deed, he was nevertheless convicted of being an accomplice to the crime and went to prison for a very long time. He apparently had no idea what was going on as he sat in the car alone. But he was guilty by association. His entire life changed in an instant because of the company he was keeping.

"Bad company corrupts good morals" is an axiom as old as mankind itself, or so it would seem. The old saying reflects a truth known far and wide, taught by parents, and recorded in holy writ.

It is not often that a person of high moral character keeping company with a person of questionable character will be able to pull the latter up to the former's level. Usually it's the other way around. The trend of fallen mankind is to take the easiest path, and the sinful nature is constantly trying to pull a person down into the depths of depravity. Life is a series of choices to either give in to or resist this pull. And a person more successfully resists temptation's call when keeping company with other people who are straining toward the higher mark.

The opposite is also true. A person will find it much easier to move toward the magnetic pull of compromise if company is being kept with chronic compromisers.

Before I elaborate in this point I feel I must first make a qualifying remark. There are hidden pitfalls in this principle of seeking out the company only of people of high moral character. The first pitfall is that of elitism and pride; seeing one's self as superior to certain unsavory people who must be shunned. The second possible pitfall is the refusal to rub shoulders with certain people who could indeed benefit from your influence. Let's remember that Jesus Himself never refused a dinner invitation from hypocrites and society's despised citizens. But He did so because He was on a mission, and His powerful strength of character kept Him unstained.

Of course, a person must do all he or she can to avoid pride and elitism by always remembering that we all struggle in areas that would disqualify us as people of high moral character in some circles, I suppose. Everyone is at different levels in their character development. And we must also remember that if we are followers of Christ, then we have been called into this world as "salt" and "light" to a world steeped in darkness. We cannot be light if we do not have associations with people who are in the darkness once in a while.

While it is not a good idea to keep close and frequent company with people of questionable character, it is nevertheless important to have friendly acquaintances along these lines. These interactions may lead to positive influences. I have friends myself who have worldviews, beliefs, and behaviors that do not match my own. But in each of those friendships, each party knows where the other stands. Those friends know who I am, what I believe, and what I will and will not do. And they know I will not budge. I enjoy their company, and they mine, but in all cases I do not keep close and frequent company with people who are immoral carousers, for example. It would be too easy for them to drag me down to their level rather than the other way around. And I certainly don't allow myself to frequent circles of people whose lifestyles are an affront to holiness and high character if I can help it. I try not to allow myself to be in social situations where I am outnumbered, if possible. There is strength in numbers.

Be Cautious in Friendship

It is said that a person is known by the company he keeps. In other words, if you want to know what kind of person someone is, just look at his or her circle of friends. Most of the time that's all you need to know. A person who wishes to maintain a stellar reputation in the community will be very choosy and even cautious in friendship.

It is always a good principle of life to try to make friends of people who are on a higher level than you so that a little of what they have rubs off. But if those kinds of people are few and far between, then at least choose friends who are on or near the same level as you for the most part, granting the few exceptions where you will be the one trying to help out someone else on a lower level than you. On this point, don't be misled by limiting your friendships to people who are close to your own age. It is difficult to find people who are significantly farther along in life than you within your own age group. Don't be afraid to initiate friendships with people who are much older and wiser.

I have a good friend, Dr. Jerry King, who is 28 years my senior. I marvel at his knowledge and wisdom. I enjoy spending time with him because I always learn from him, and I always feel challenged by his example and see myself in a truer and more humble light when I am with him. It's very easy to think more highly of one's self than we should. But when in the presence of someone obviously greater, more accomplished and more knowledgeable, it tends to bring us back down to earth.

Dr. King, however, has had to stoop down a little in order to be my friend. There is very little I can offer him in terms of enrichment, except for the fact that he finds an eager student in me, and I'm sure that is gratifying. He has had to be willing to go out of his way in order to answer my questions and to spend time helping me come up to a higher level. But again, I am an eager student and not someone who resists being taught. He and I are kindred spirits, though far apart in terms of knowledge and personal development. He knows there is benefit to him in sowing into my life because he will reap from it in time in some way, and I know there is benefit to me by allowing him to.

For Christian young people, I offer this one last clarification on this point: It is possible to settle for the "good" and miss the "best."

I have witnessed Christian young people who hang out together who instead of helping each other in the fight against temptation, will instead simply pool their compromise. In other words, they may have avoided the pitfalls of being closely associated with obviously immoral people, and that's good, but they have instead surrounded themselves with people who are nevertheless compromisers in less obvious and more sociably acceptable ways, and thus, they miss out on the best.

The compromise I see most often in even some church-going people is in three major areas primarily: their language (profanity), their viewing and listening habits, and their loose standards on alcohol consumption. It is very disappointing to me when I hear about church-going people who talk like sailors, who listen to music and watch movies that are full of horror and immorality, and who haunt bars and slam down whiskey shots like any party animal would. It makes me wonder if they have any Christian standards at all. Rather than taking the moral high road of behavior that is above reproach and obeying First Thessalonians 5:22 by avoiding even the *appearance* of evil, they have rationalized doing what the immoral do and inhabiting places where the immoral gather. They, too, are guilty by association.

A person cannot maintain a good witness for Christ while doing what the immoral do and gathering where the immoral gather. I was taught this lesson the night I decided to go to a bar with some of my college classmates just to have a beer or two and enjoy their company. By this time I had come back to the Lord after a long prodigal journey, and I was serious about my walk with the Lord. I rationalized going to the bar because it was not my intention to get drunk or pick up women. I was just there to enjoy the people. As I sat there nursing a beer, one young lady who was in my math class walked by my table and stopped in her tracks when she saw me. "Wow," she said. "I didn't expect to see *you* here." You see, I had already been a witness for Christ in my college class, and this young lady knew where I stood on spiritual matters. And she expressed dismay that I would be hanging out in a place where people were getting drunk and picking up one-night stands. Although we had never discussed alcohol or bar-hopping, she apparently expected more from me than what she saw that night. Although I wasn't doing anything immoral, in her mind I was compromising and apparently guilty by association. Her words pierced my heart, and I have not been in a bar since.

I counsel you to always strive for the high road in everything, and choose friends who will walk that road with you. Be aware that even "Christian" people can be terribly shallow, self-centered, and worldly in many respects. Choose your friends carefully if you want to rise high in life.

>*Abstain from all appearance of evil.*
>-*1 Thessalonians 5:22* (KJV)

>*"The righteous person is cautious in his friendship, but the way of the wicked leads them astray."*
>-*Proverbs 12:26* (NET)

"Whoever walks with the wise becomes wise, but the companion of fools will suffer harm."
-**Proverbs 13:20** (ESV)

"To be of good quality, you have to excuse yourself from the presence of shallow and callow minded individuals."
- *Michael Bassey Johnson*

"Plantations of good morals are easily captivated, colonized and corrupted by the pests of bad company. Spray away bad companies and you will experience a bumper harvest of your dream fruits!"
-*Israelmore Ayivor*

19

Swimming Upstream

In 2012 the Nightingale Conant group, a publisher of success-related personal growth materials, published a book called, **The Top 2%**. The back cover reads, *"The top 2% sets the trends in every industry. They set the trends by imagining and dreaming things that didn't exist and then doing what it took to make it happen. Whether you're in business, entertainment, sports, politics, or some other industry, if you're in the top 2%, you have the power and influence to make things happen."*

It has become easier to succeed these days in some respects, since we live in a culture of people who have become increasingly influenced by an attitude of entitlement, and fewer people are willing to make the sacrifices necessary to rise to the tops of their professions. As late motivational speaker and author, Zig Ziglar, was known to say, "There's plenty of room at the top."

Shooting for the top 2%, however, should not be relegated to business, although I certainly recommend striving to rise to the top in your profession. It seems to be true in every aspect of life that the masses will tend to do what's always been done, do what feels good now, make few sacrifices, and pander to their comforts and lusts. Thus, many people stay right where they are and never progress in life. Once people graduate from high school, many of them stop learning and settle in to a life of familiarity, comfort, and mediocrity. While no specific percentages or numbers can be applied to this assertion, this certainly seems to be the case much of the time.

Stop and think for a moment about what mediocrity means: *It means being the best of the worst, and the worst of the best.* It means being neither terrible nor great. And let me tell you something: no one pays for mediocrity. No one pays money to go see a mediocre performer, for example. They pay money to go see someone extraordinary.

Even the Bible speaks of doing what you do with all your might:

> *"Whatever you do, whether in word or deed, do it all in the name of the Lord Jesus, giving thanks to God the Father through Him."*
> *-Colossians 3:17* (NIV)

For the disciple of Jesus Christ, Colossians 3:17 represents the motive for why we strive to be the best and rise above the masses: it's because we are living our lives as thank offerings to God Who saved us through Jesus Christ. And in order to bring glory to His Name, we live on purpose, striving to glorify Him in everything we do, large and small.

If you want to be good at life, one fundamental principle is to simply look around at what the majority of society is doing, and then go the other way. If you follow the crowd, you may end up running with them over the edge of the cliff. It takes someone of unique strength to resist the temptation to go along with everyone else.

My wife and I seem to have been called by God to separate ourselves from the crowd in a number of ways. In several areas of our lives we are the object of derision among relatives and some acquaintances. We are homeschoolers, we take supplements, eat fairly clean and avoid fast food, we try to avoid conventional medicine for the most, and, of course, we serve the Lord Jesus Christ passionately and not passively. Even among some groups of Christians we are the odd balls. We believe God wants to bless His people and that Christians are not supposed to go through life constantly defeated and frustrated. That philosophy alone puts us in the minority of Christians, since many of our brethren seem to believe that constant pain and struggle is how God has called us to live. While suffering is certainly part of the Christian experience, so is victory!

> *"Many are the afflictions of the righteous, but*
> *the LORD delivers him out of them all."*
> *-Psalm 34:19* (NIV)

Swimming upstream has become a way of life for my wife and me. But that is fine with us because we are striving to be the best we can be, and the most successful people, including Christians, will strive against the flow of society much of the time. We are strangers and aliens in this world (1 Peter 2:11). And if you wish to follow Christ, or even wish to rise to the top 2% in your profession, you will find yourself in the minority a lot: in political views, in social issues, etc. But don't let being a minority concern you. If being extraordinary was easy, everyone would be doing it! And then no one would be extraordinary!

> *"Enter through the narrow gate. For wide is the*
> *gate and broad is the road that leads to destruction,*
> *and many enter through it. But small is the gate and*
> *narrow the road that leads to life, and only a few*
> *find it."*
> *-Jesus, from Matthew 7:13-14* (NIV)

> *"Whenever you find yourself on the side of the*
> *majority, it is time to pause and reflect." -Mark*
> *Twain*

20

An Excellent Spirit

Exceed expectations.

That concept has been adopted by some companies, but not very many individuals. It seems the habit of most people is to do barely enough to get by. Many employees do just enough to keep their bosses off their backs, but don't seem to care too much about delighting their bosses by exceeding expectations.

I sent an electronic device in for repair recently. I expected to receive the product back within a week or so, but it arrived at my door in a day and half. I was amazed and delighted. But then I discovered that two of the three issues that I sent the device in for were unresolved. Needless to say, my delight waned when I discovered the incomplete job.

Many people live by a double standard of sorts. They want people to meet or exceed their expectations when they have never put the effort in to exceeding the expectations of those around them. And life doesn't work that way. You reap what you sow. If you sow into the lives of others by working to exceed what they expect of you, life will pay you back in kind.

If you borrow someone's car, for example, and it is loaned to you a little dusty and with a half tank of gas in it, return it with a full tank of gas and a car wash.

If your teacher or professor asks you to submit a written report, don't just give him words on paper. Dress it up by placing it in a clear view binder and attaching an attractive title page.

If your boss asks you to complete a certain project, try to get it done before he or she expects it, and then eagerly ask what else you can do for him or her.

If your wife asks you to pick up your socks, consider tidying up a little in other areas as well. It will delight her! And she may exceed your expectations in other ways that delight you!

Look for unexpected ways to delight those around you. It will not only make their lives happier, but it will make yours happier, too. And it will most certainly boost your career and relationships.

Another way to articulate the concept of exceeding expectations is to simply endeavor to be a person of uncompromised excellence in everything you do – *everything!*

I learned that life skill from my father, Bob Robbins. My dad was and still is a man of excellence. He exceeded his customer's expectations in his business, and whatever he set out to do, he did it with amazing attention to detail. Dad for most of his life was a piano tuner and and rebuilder by trade. I worked for him for a few years learning the trade when I was in my teens and early twenties, and I learned how to rebuild a piano from the ground up. I never did it as well as he did only because I don't have the natural mechanical prowess he does, but I nevertheless learned the fine art of excellence from his high standards of workmanship that he demanded of himself and those who worked for him. I remember that whenever we were putting new finishes on pianos, my dad demanded that we spruce up the appearance of the backsides and underneath sides as well. These were the parts of a piano that no one ever really saw for the most part. But Dad considered a refinishing job incomplete until these areas were refurbished as well. To say that my dad was maniacal about excellence would not be an understatement. But it paid him dividends. No one had a better reputation in central Indiana for piano work than my dad.

The Virtues of Orderliness and Cleanliness

Let me take a bit of a side journey here and explain two important reasons why tidiness is an important aspect of excellence and good stewardship as well.

First, a tidy home, office and car is a better organized and more efficient home, office and car. I can't count the number of times I have misplaced things because my bedroom or office or car have been so cluttered and disorganized. I have wasted an untold amount of time looking for items that I eventually found dropped in a corner on the floor or tucked away under a pile of clutter. Tidiness has not come naturally for me because of the way my brain works, I guess, and because I was never required by my late mother to keep a tidy room and living space growing up. My parents were divorced when I was very young, and my dad's house was always immaculate. But since I didn't live with him, I did not have the opportunity to learn from his example on a day-to-day basis. And now as an adult, I understand why my dad was so meticulous about tidiness. Tidiness is another form of excellence, and it's a heck of a lot more efficient!

I remember accepting the invitation to visit a family's home some time ago. There was some clutter laying around the foyer area as Donna and I walked in; nothing too offensive, but it was definitely noticeable. But then when I visited their restroom, I was a bit taken aback. The place looked like it hadn't been cleaned in a month. There was grime in the sink, and the toilet had tell-tale traces of someone's bowel movement stuck in the bottom of the bowl and was lined with grime on the rim. I thought to myself that surely these nice folks could have had the foresight to know that their guests would need to use the restroom while we were there. Could they not have invested ten minutes in making the bathroom presentable before we visited? It wasn't like they had a major plumbing problem or something that was difficult to address. A toilet brush and a rag would have remedied the problem in a few minutes. But apparently they did not consider the concept of honoring their guests by removing any potentially uncomfortable or unsightly surroundings.

I must hasten to add here that I do not feel I have arrived in the area of orderliness, but I'm making strides forward. As a homeschooling family with kids constantly underfoot, Donna and I have had to compromise in some areas and prioritize what's most important. That has meant that keeping a perfectly tidy house is not always possible or even reasonable at times. The same has gone for maintaining a career and a ministry simultaneously. At some point, something has to give. However, we have at least given our guests the honor of tidying up and making our home more than presentable for company.

From a spiritual perspective, tidiness is part of faithfulness and good stewardship. It is a mark of responsible character to take care of that which God has given, and that goes for one's house, car, money, clothes, appearance, and even one's body and health. How can we expect God to bless us with more if we don't even take care of the things we now have? How can we expect people to take us seriously if we always have an untidy, disheveled appearance, or everything about our possessions and surroundings screams negligence, shabbiness, carelessness and irresponsibility?

Again, exceeding expectations and being a person of excellence must begin at home as a matter of lifestyle, and as this is lived out from day to day, it will spill out onto other important aspects of our lives on the job and in ministry.

On a side note, I should hasten to add that some people are not naturally given to orderliness. It was said of Beethoven, for example, that he kept a very disorderly and untidy home because so much of his energies went to honing his musical craft that he didn't care about anything else. Beethoven's focus on his work is why we are still talking about him today, because he became amazing. So if you are a Beethoven in the making, someone who is so focused on honing your craft that orderliness eludes you, well, I applaud that focus. But allow me to remind you that

Beethoven never married, so he didn't have a wife to think about. He could keep his home as unkempt as he wanted, and no one except maybe a few guests would care. Beethoven was a master composer, but he wasn't especially good at life. What we should be seeking to achieve is some sort of balance, and if that means you have to hire a housekeeper or an office assistant to do what you cannot do because you do not have the skills, time, or energy to do it, fine. In fact, I think it is a very good idea to hire other people to take care of the things we cannot do ourselves but that we should nevertheless be giving some attention to, such as organization.

The Spiritual Significance of the Spirit of Excellence

Is excellence truly a spiritual quality? If the lives of Joseph and Daniel are any indication, we would have to resoundingly and emphatically answer yes!

Even a cursory reading of the latter chapters of Genesis demonstrate that Joseph was a man of great integrity and excellence in everything he did. And the results were evident in his life. God could trust him with little, so Joseph was eventually entrusted with great responsibility, wealth, and power.

As for Daniel, the sixth chapter of the book of Daniel says of him,

> **Then this Daniel was preferred above the presidents and princes, because an excellent spirit was in him; and the king thought to set him over the whole realm.** (vs. 6, KJV)

Daniel's spirit of excellence was associated with his level of godliness. In fact, the excellence he pursued in his spiritual life – what we could call integrity – put him on a course for the excellence he demonstrated in matters of administration and government to make him a very important figure under three separate kings. Daniel went above and beyond the call of duty in his service to those rulers. He did *more* than what was expected of him, and it distinguished him above all the other dignitaries of that time and place.

Doing more than what is expected of you is a principle taught by our Lord Jesus. It was He Who said, *"If anyone forces you to go one mile, go with him two."* (Matthew 54:1)

Elegance and Beauty are a Part of Excellence

It is common in today's church world to exalt the virtue of humility. This is an important quality, to be sure. However, in the pursuit of humility many people mistakenly believe that they must desire a drabness in their dress and possessions, giving little or no thought to elegance and the pleasantness of their appearance, surroundings and belongings.

In the pursuit of humility there is a danger in going too far in the other direction and becoming so dull and/or disheveled that it draws attention to itself, which violates the entire goal of humility. The Amish, for example, in attempting to avoid any dress that could be considered vain and ostentatious go so far in the other direction that their manner of dress stands out starkly against the rest of the world, and that, too, draws attention to itself. While I am certainly a strong proponent of keeping one's self sufficiently covered in the goal of humble attire and not going overboard with expensive jewelry and extravagant clothing, I am also a strong proponent of looking sharp, professional, and adorning one's self in such a way as to not bring dishonor to one's reputation or the reputation of our Savior. If people cannot take you seriously because of your appearance, then that is going to affect your career, relationships, and witness for Christ.

Some people have also adopted the attitude that the appearance and condition of their homes and possessions are of little importance. As stated before, taking care of that with which God has blessed us is an issue of stewardship, but it could also legitimately be argued that beauty and elegance are godly characteristics. Let us not forget that God gave Moses very specific instructions about the construction and beautification of the Tabernacle. Its appearance was to be a representation of the glory of God, and therefore it was to be exceedingly magnificent. God obviously likes beauty and elegance. Have you ever read how elaborate the Temple in Jerusalem was that Solomon built, or of the mind-blowing extravagance of Heaven?

There is nothing about God that hints of cheapness or shabbiness. And while our *highest* aims as Christians should not be focused on outward adornment or trappings, it is nevertheless a mark of godliness to do the very best with what you have. Keep an orderly home decorated pleasantly; keep your car well maintained and clean; cloth yourself in attire that, even when you are casual, models good taste and respectability. In everything you do and own, do as Daniel did and be known for a spirit of excellence.

Yes, excellence in all the various forms it takes is a spiritual quality. A cluttered life riddled with traces of low standards of quality is evidence of what is likely happening on the inside of a person as well, at least to some degree. While it's possible to have high standards of quality in one's work and environment but still be a wreck emotionally and spiritually, I have found that people who are healthy spiritually will show evidence of that outwardly as well. That's why 3 John 1:2 says, *"Beloved, I wish above all things that you may prosper and be in health, **even as your soul prospers**."* Inward health will ultimately demonstrate itself outwardly.

Excellence begins on the inside, and it should be working its way out and showing up on the outside as well in the form of good planning, attention to detail, orderliness and elegance, and exceeding the expectations of others.

*"²The Lord was with Joseph so that he prospered,
and he lived in the house of his Egyptian master.*

³When his master saw that the Lord was with him and that the Lord gave him success in everything he did, ⁴Joseph found favor in his eyes and became his attendant. Potiphar put him in charge of his household, and he entrusted to his care everything he owned. ⁵From the time he put him in charge of his household and of all that he owned, the Lord blessed the household of the Egyptian because of Joseph. The blessing of the Lord was on everything Potiphar had, both in the house and in the field. ⁶So Potiphar left everything he had in Joseph's care; with Joseph in charge, he did not concern himself with anything except the food he ate."

    -Genesis 39:2-6 (NIV)

"The quality of a person's life is in direct proportion to their commitment to excellence, regardless of their chosen field of endeavor."

    -Vince Lombardi

"It's when ordinary people rise above the expectations and seize the opportunity that milestones truly are reached."

    –Mike Huckabee

"Cleanliness may be defined to be the emblem of purity of mind."

    -Joseph Addison

"Plan your progress carefully; hour-by-hour, day-by-day, month-by-month. Organized activity and maintained enthusiasm are the wellsprings of your power."

    -Paul Meyer

"Excellence is the gradual result of always striving to do better."
-Pat Riley

"If a man is called to be a street sweeper, he should sweep streets even as Michelangelo painted, or Beethoven composed music, or Shakespeare wrote poetry. He should sweep streets so well that all the hosts of heaven and earth will pause to say, here lived a great street sweeper who did his job well."
-Martin Luther King, Jr.

"Today, and every day, deliver more than you are getting paid to do. The victory of success will be half won when you learn the secret of putting out more than is expected in all that you do. Make yourself so valuable in your work that eventually you will become indispensable. Exercise your privilege to go the extra mile, and enjoy all the rewards you receive. You deserve them!"
-Og Mandino

21

What Got You There Won't Keep You There

One day a field marshal requested an audience with Napoleon, and the great military commander agreed to hear him out. The field marshal brought a report of a great victory he had led. He talked on and on about his accomplishment, while Napoleon listened closely but said nothing. The officer was disheartened. He had hoped for a more enthusiastic response, as well as, perhaps, congratulations from his commander. He received neither.

The officer summed up by repeating much of what he had already detailed. When he had finally concluded his discourse, Napoleon asked him this question: "What did you do the next day?"

The officer was dumbstruck. But the lesson was not lost on him. The field marshal understood that he should never rest on his laurels and congratulate himself for yesterday's accomplishments. From then on he left it to others to bequeath whatever acclaim might be due him.

The origins of the phrase, "resting on one's laurels," lie in ancient Greece, where laurel wreaths were symbols of victory and status. Its meaning refers to a person who, after achieving high success, begins to rely on the momentum of that success instead of continuing to work toward future successes. It suggests the tendency to be satisfied with one's past success and to consider further effort unnecessary, and hence, to decline into laziness and lack of application.

Accomplishment and success are wonderful things, but if you are not careful they will breed a tendency to back off the accelerator and ease into cruise control. The danger of this tendency is that, to quote a popular axiom, "What got you there won't keep you there." In other words, whatever it took to excel in your chosen field won't be what keeps you at an elite level. You must constantly hone and build upon your skills, re-invent yourself to keep up with the changing work environment, and even discover new skills. The work force now is very competitive, and it is only people who are willing to continue bettering themselves who enjoy lasting success.

There are plenty of stories of flash-in-the-pan successes in business, one-hit-wonders in music, and one-and-done champions in sports. In the field of professional sports, for example, it is very rare for a championship team to repeat as champion the following year. It happens occasionally, but not often. Part of the reason is that when the pinnacle of success is reached, the fire inside cools a little. What got that team to the championship level doesn't keep them there most of the time. Even the great NBA team, The Golden State Warriors, who won their first championship in 2015, and who cruised to a record-setting regular season mark of 73-9 the following year, were surprised in the 2016 championship series when a hungrier Cleveland Cavaliers team came from behind to overcome a 3-1 deficit and to win out and defeat a team that many thought were the best in history. Similarly, the Chicago Cubs baseball team, which won the World Series in 2016 and enjoyed the best record in baseball that season, responded the very next year by barely being able to keep their winning average above .500 much of the year, and they eventually fell short in the playoffs. Indeed, what got you there won't always keep you there!

The wise person continues to push the envelope and is in a constant mode of learning, developing, and growing. The wise person also understands that going the extra mile and continuing to develop even after a certain level of success has been reached will not be noticed or appreciated by everyone, at least at first. Much of what we do to reach and sustain success is done in private where no one sees. It's the reading and study, the intellectual and spiritual development done in secret that only you and God know about for which no one pats you on the back. But it is the result of that diligence that gets you noticed and rewarded.

I fully acknowledge that study and training is not usually fun. In fact, it's often tedious, boring and frustrating. It is the eventual outcome of those sacrifices, however, that will make or break your future. As Muhammad Ali once said, "I hated every minute of training. But I said, 'Don't quit. Suffer now and live the rest of your life as a champion.'"

"Diligent hands will rule, but laziness ends in forced labor."
   -Proverbs 12:24 (NIV)

"[24]Do you not know that in a race all the runners run, but only one gets the prize? Run in such a way as to get the prize. [25]Everyone who competes in the games goes into strict training. They do it to get a crown that will not last, but we do it to get a crown that will last forever. [26]Therefore I do not run like someone running aimlessly; I do not fight like a boxer beating the air. [27]No, I strike a blow to my body and make it my slave so that after I have preached to others, I myself will not be disqualified for the prize."
   -1 Corinthians 9:24-27 (NIV)

"Successful and unsuccessful people do not vary greatly in their abilities. They vary in their desires to reach their potential."
- John Maxwell

22

Don't Be Ruled by Anything

If there's one gigantic thing that will undermine your progress in life, it's addiction. No matter how talented or knowledgeable a person might be, he or she cannot excel in life ruled by an addiction, because the addiction is in charge, and the person victimized by it is not. That's why the Bible says to not allow yourself to be ruled by anything.

Addiction to drugs and alcohol, are, of course, the most life-altering of all addictions because of how they drain finances, dry up motivation, and alter one's judgment. A person addicted to mind-altering substances will utterly ruin his or her life. I have witnessed it firsthand numerous times. Addiction never fails to be ruinous.

The majority of people in our society know enough about how devastating addiction can be that they know to avoid it. It's important, however, to consider that the drug addict didn't start out thinking he was going to be an addict. The alcoholic didn't wake up one day and think to herself, "I have an idea: I think I'll start binge drinking today and shoot for all-out alcoholism in a few months." No one thinks those kinds of thoughts. The addict slips into the addiction unnoticed, numb to the insidious effects of the addiction taking hold little by little. It all started with an "innocent" experimental toke. It began as a curiosity about how a wine "buzz" feels. And when something feels that good, what's the harm in indulging now and then? Right? It is that lack of watchfulness over one's appetites that is the downfall of countless people.

In this hedonistic society, however, addictions don't stop at drugs and alcohol. Illicit sex is a major addictive behavior. People – particularly men – who are addicted to the high of casual sexual encounters often find themselves enslaved to something shallow and ultimately unfulfilling, but somehow they cannot make themselves stop, even if they get married. Their perversion follows them relentlessly, and it usually wrecks any hope of a lasting and fulfilling marriage. The ultimate outcome that often accompanies unchecked sexual or emotional lust (the latter of which refers to a constant exorbitant craving for validation), is adultery, which has been the ruin of countless families since time began I suppose. Some of the strongest and lengthiest warnings in the Bible have to do with the life-torpedoing after-effects of adultery (see Proverbs, chapters 5, 6, and 7).

Listen to the stern warning in Proverbs 6:

> *[26]For a prostitute can be had for a loaf of bread, but another man's wife preys on your very life. [27]Can a man scoop fire into his lap without his clothes being burned? [28]Can a man walk on hot coals without his feet being scorched? [29]So is he who sleeps with another man's wife; no one who touches her will go unpunished.* (NIV)

Adultery is almost always devastating on marriages and families, but the monsters of sexual addictions loose in our world today have taken on new forms. They will no longer settle for being confined to singles bars, college fraternities, and the beds of those caught up in the tentacles of adultery. Neither are they content to be relegated to sleazy bookstores, strip bars, or call girls for hire. They have made their way right into people's homes – good homes with happy families. And it is there that sons and husbands – and even, in some cases, wives and daughters – have succumbed to the hypnotizing siren songs of pornography.

It is said that pornography is a harder habit to break than cocaine addiction. Similar to the drug addict, probably, the user feels shame and disgust at himself when he comes down off his erotic high. He may even hate himself. But he goes right back again, driven by an appetite he can neither understand nor control. And he has become oh-so-good at hiding it. Well, many men have anyway. Some have been caught red-handed by their wives or parents, much to the agony of the family members who discover it. It has ruined marriages, ministries, and even careers.

I sat across the desk from a man who came to me looking for help to somehow repair the damage he had done to his marriage with pornography. I vividly remember how he looked, his red face wet with tears and contorted with the torment of what was happening to his marriage. If only he could go back in time and undo everything. But he could not. This was his new reality, and he had to own it.

Even if a pornography addiction is never discovered by family members, it nevertheless sucks the enjoyment and fulfilment out of life. It prevents true intimacy with one's spouse. A dark cloud of shame, guilt and embarrassment comes with it, and that shame is amplified 100-fold in the life of a Christian. In people's heart of hearts, they know pornography is wrong. And in the life of the Christian, he knows it is indeed evil. That is the gut-wrenching dilemma of porn addiction: The Christian feels powerless and overpowered by something wicked that has engulfed him. He swears he will never do it again, but he does. He can no longer keep track of all the times he has promised himself and God that he will stop and then gone right back to it. Sometimes he feels nauseated at himself.

Of course, an ounce of prevention is worth a pound of cure, the old saying goes. It is so much easier to have never touched the deviant, addictive stuff in the first place rather than to have to fight one battle after another trying to rid one's self of the various demonic parasites that attach themselves to people. That is part of the message of this chapter: *don't go near the source of temptation*. Don't touch it. Don't look in its direction. Don't be in the same room with it. Don't even be in the same part of town with it if you can help it. By doing so you will save yourself so much pain, so much effort. Obey the advice of Proverbs about even going near the source of temptation:

> **⁷Now then, my sons, listen to me; do not turn aside from what I say. ⁸Keep to a path far from her [or it], do not go near the door of her house, ⁹lest you lose your honor to others and your dignity to one who is cruel, ¹⁰lest strangers feast on your wealth and your toil enrich the house of another. ¹¹At the end of your life you will groan, when your flesh and body are spent. ¹²You will say, "How I hated discipline! How my heart spurned correction! ¹³I would not obey my teachers or turn my ear to my instructors."**
> **-Proverbs 5:6-13** (NIV)

However, many people are already beyond the prevention stage. Many people are already addicted to something, and statistics show that the most common addiction of all is now enslavement to pornography. There's something about it; the effect it has on the dopamine pathways of the brain that makes it practically irresistible even in the lives of men who know better and who want better.

So the second part of the message of this chapter is directed to those who find themselves addicted to pornography or a chemical substance, and that message is to not make the mistake of thinking you can control this thing easily. That is the mistake that many people with a porn addiction make. "Yeah, I've stumbled a few times, but I'm through with it. It's no big deal." They make that mistake because they don't crave it every day like a heroin addict might crave his next fix. Weeks might go by without using pornography, but it always seems to find a way to creep back in. Before long ten years have gone by and the user doesn't remember a time when he has gone longer than a couple of months without using. It might not be a daily addiction, but it's an addiction nevertheless, and its sucking the zest for life right of him.

My advice is to gouge out your eye and cut off your hand. Not literally, of course, but figuratively. Jesus said if your hand offends you, cut if off and throw it away. And if your eye offends you, gouge it out and throw it away, because it would better to go into eternity without a hand or an eye than to go into hell intact (see Matthew 18:8-9). That means be radical about freeing yourself from your addiction. If you have to get rid of your smartphone and go with a flip phone with no internet, do it. If you have to get rid of your computer or TV, do it. Or if you have to cut off friendships in order to avoid being near certain temptations, then it's worth it.

You also need the support of a friend or two; people who can look in on you, ask you the tough questions, hold you accountable, and provide support when things are tough. Don't be too proud to seek out help. Believe me, no one will think less of you because you are looking for help. In the case of lust and pornography, many men are secretly dealing with the same thing. Finding a sympathetic friend isn't too difficult.

Ultimately, while all of these methods are good, they still only address the symptom of a disease lying beneath the surface. That disease will only resurface if one addresses merely symptoms. Addiction is a symptom, and **the disease is a sin nature hell-bent on pleasing itself. Without a heart broken before God that is willing to acknowledge the repulsively self-centered nature of its sinful condition, your addictions will likely remain attached to you.** You must seek God out like your life depends on it because, friend, in some respects your life DOES depend on it. And only in the light of His glorious presence daily sought out can you hope to be free from that thing that has now become a part of your very personality. Freedom is possible, but not on your own. Personal barriers, repentance, the support of friends, and seeking after the God Who knows you better than you know yourself is your only hope.

Addiction is one of the biggest and most widespread problems in our society, and yes, even in the church. Research shows that 68% of men in church watch porn on a regular basis. It's obvious that just trying harder is not the answer. There are principles for victory, but discussing them in detail would be too lengthy in a book like this. So allow me to make a recommendation. *The Conquer Series: The Battle Plan for Sexual Purity,* is a 5-hour DVD training by Dr. Ted Roberts that is designed to target heart transformation, not just behavior modification. Dr. Roberts' training is designed to teach men the weapons and strategies of God to get free from sexual addiction and prevent relapse. The series can be found at ConquerSeries.com. The book by C. Matthew McMahon, *Overcoming Lust,* is also excellent.

If you are struggling with an addiction or a particular area of sin, training like what the Conquer Series offers could be your answer, particularly if your addiction is of a sexual nature. But the following verses and quotes may also provide some strength for the battle.

"¹¹...count yourselves dead to sin but alive to God in Christ Jesus. ¹²Therefore do not let sin reign in your mortal body so that you obey its evil desires. ¹³Do not offer any part of yourself to sin as an instrument of wickedness, but rather offer yourselves to God as those who have been brought from death to life; and offer every part of yourself to him as an

instrument of righteousness. [16]Don't you know that when you offer yourselves to someone as obedient slaves, you are slaves of the one you obey—whether you are slaves to sin, which leads to death, or to obedience, which leads to righteousness?"
    -Romans 6:11-13, 16 (NIV)

"Sin is crouching at your door; it desires to have you, but you must master it."
    –Genesis 4:7b (NIV)

"Like a dog that returns to his vomit is a fool who repeats his folly."
    –Proverbs 26:11 (NIV)

"I will be conduct myself wisely in a blameless way... I will walk with integrity within my house. I will set no vile thing before my eyes."
    –Psalm 101:2-3 (NIV)

"I made a covenant with my eyes not to look lustfully upon a girl. Does He not see my ways and count my every step?"
    -Job 31:1, 4 (NIV)

"Like a muddied spring or a polluted well is a righteous man who gives way to the wicked."
    –Proverbs 25:26 (NIV)

"Like a city with broken down walls is a man who lacks self-control."
    –Proverbs 25:28 (NIV)

[3]It is God's will that you should be sanctified: that you should avoid sexual immorality; [4]that each of you should learn to control your own body in a

way that is holy and honorable, 5 not in passionate lust like the pagans, who do not know God; 6 and that in this matter no one should wrong or take advantage of a brother or sister. The Lord will punish all those who commit such sins, as we told you and warned you before. 7For God did not call us to be impure, but to live a holy life. 8 Therefore, anyone who rejects this instruction does not reject a human being but God, the very God who gives you his Holy Spirit."

-1 Thessalonians 4:3-8 (NIV)

"Wine produces mockers; alcohol leads to brawls. Those led away by drink cannot be wise."

-Proverbs 20:1 (NLT)

"Sex without love is absolutely ridiculous."
-Sophia Loren

"Our greatest glory is not in never failing, but in rising up every time we fail."
– Ralph Waldo Emerson

23

How to Direct Your Passion

One of the most important things you will do in your entire life is to find your passion, something for which you feel you were born.

When you find your passion, life takes on purpose and significance. You will find your path and stay on that path and more easily endure all kinds of adversity in staying the course. People who do not have a purpose will easily give up when the slightest difficulty presents itself. Thus, they never really progress much in life.

Many times your passion will translate into money. The thing you are most passionate about will often forge a path toward a successful and enjoyable career. As has been said, "Do what you love, and the money will follow."

I would add a qualifier to that axiom. I would go on to say to do what you love, and if it doesn't make money for you, then do what you love in serving mankind.

You see, not everyone who has a passion is able to make money at it. People who are passionate about evangelism, for example, will work a job they don't like that much but do it joyfully because they are doing it to help fund their missionary work. Some people who are passionate about their sport of choice cannot always reach the professional level for a variety of reasons, but they will then use their love of the sport to coach and teach other athletes and help build character in youngsters. Although they may not have landed a mega-contract with a professional sports team, their knowledge and love of the sport is still serving a purpose, and there is pleasure and fulfillment in that. And churches around the world are occupied by excellent musicians and singers who are not able to make a decent living at music, but they are nevertheless enjoying playing music and serving an important purpose while doing it.

Similarly, your passion and purpose in life may not be about a career at all, but about being instrumental in bringing positive change to an ongoing wrong or social plague of some sort. For example, some people's lives seem to be driven by an injustice that they see in our society and which causes them great personal pain or frustration, such as abortion or sex trafficking, and they are very involved in efforts to eradicate these things from our society. Others are driven by the plight of the impoverished and are always finding ways to reach out to the poor and relieve their suffering in some way. While God will help each person who follows Him to find their niche in the realm of business, God will also likely lay on your heart a passion for a particular area of need in our world that needs your involvement.

In finding your life purpose, there is also an important component of allowing yourself to be flexible while finding it. Be open to new possibilities and paths you had not considered.

When I entered the world of business, for example, I was not very good at anything that might be considered in high demand in the marketplace. My passion was music, but I was never able to make a living at it. Health and physical fitness was another passion of mine, and I found myself often playing the part of an evangelist for better health, wanting to help people to reach their potential and overcome illness. So when I was job hunting shortly after getting married, the job opportunity that piqued my interest the most was a position selling holistic medicine health products to doctors. Although I did not consider myself a sales person, and although I did not feel I had the kind of professional skills in the marketplace that would land me the position, the CEO nevertheless saw me as qualified based upon my passion for health and fitness, and he hired me. The rest is history. I went on to become one of the most successful people in the company, not because I am unusually talented as a sales person, but simply because I believe so much in what I do and have a passion to help people. A passion to help people is a success principle, too. As Zig Ziglar, once said, "You can have everything you want if you will just help enough people get what they want."

That is so true. Life is about serving. If you can find a way to serve mankind with your passion, one way or another you are going to find fulfillment and success, even if it doesn't come in the form you expected.

Joseph in the Bible found that out the hard way. In his youth, he had dreams of grandeur. Then life got hard – very hard. But as he continued to serve excellently wherever he found himself, eventually his passion to help people combined with the skills and knowledge he had acquired landed him the second most important position in the entire kingdom of ancient Egypt.

So don't give up on your passion, but be open to God directing your life according to *His* purpose for creating you. Simply serve God wholeheartedly and use what He has given you to serve Him and others. And when you do, life has a way of rewarding you.

"It is the ultimate luxury to combine passion and contribution. It's also a very clear path to happiness."
-Sheryl Sandberg

"Without passion you don't have energy. Without energy you have nothing."
    -Donald Trump

"You have a choice. You should be aiming to craft something that you find rewarding and exciting.... If you do that, everything else tends to fall into place."
    –Tim Ferris

24

Activating Your Inner GPS

In the mid 1940s war-torn Japan was in a state of devastation. In an effort to rebuild their decimated nation, leaders set a goal in 1950 that they would be the number one producing country in the world of textiles in that decade. By 1959, Japan had achieved that objective. In 1960, they set another goal that they would become the number one nation in the world in the production of steel during that decade, in spite of the fact that there is no iron ore nor coal in Japan of any significance. In spite of those obstacles, they achieved that goal as well. In 1970 they set yet another goal that during the 70s Japan would become the number one nation in the world in the production of automobiles. This time they failed to make their goal within the time frame they had hoped, but they missed it by only one year, becoming the top producer of automobiles in the world in 1980. Japan has maintained its status of the number one producer of automobiles in the world ever since.

It seems clear from Japan's success in industry that goal-setting for ambitious nations consisting of millions of people working together can work miracles. But does goal setting work the same for individuals as it does nations? There are countless examples and inspirational stories that positively demonstrate the answer to that question. Ronald Reagan, in fact, lived his life by the philosophy of setting goals. He said, "My philosophy of life is that if we make up our mind what we are going to make of our lives, then work hard toward that goal, we never lose -- somehow we win out." Basketball legend Julius Erving also fittingly said, "Goals determine what you're going to be."

It has been said that if you don't know where you are going, it takes a long time to get nowhere.

There is a mysterious power in goal setting. Just as the autopilot on an airplane or the GPS in your phone or car identifies a destination then charts a course to get there, everyone appears to have an inner GPS built into us that puts us on the fast track to our destination once the destination is identified. As we discussed in the previous chapter, it's important to have even a vague life purpose or passion, and once that purpose or passion has been identified, goals can then be set in place to get you where you want to go.

A goal has to be specific. If it's too broad or vague, it doesn't get you anywhere. If your goal is simply to make a million dollars someday, that goal won't produce results in most cases because it's too vague and without a plan. You don't have a roadmap to get you there, so it's unlikely you will ever arrive at that destination. If, however, you have a specific goal to own your own consulting business, for example, and you know some details about what you are hoping to achieve, some intermediate goals to help you reach the ultimate goal, an amount of money in mind that you would like to make, and a time frame in getting there, then there's strength in that plan. You will more than likely achieve or get something close to what you envision when you have visualized the ultimate destination and have even a rough plan in getting there.

A goal also has to be realistic. It would be unrealistic, for example, to make a goal of being an NFL running back if you are fifty-years-old and fifty pounds overweight. Your goal has to be something you can absolutely achieve. It may take some work, strategy and time to get there, and it may stretch you, but it's something you can do.

I must also hasten to mention that while success gurus in the secular world tout the importance of goal setting and specificity in your goals, goal setting may look a little different for the Christian. The follower of Jesus Christ must stay flexible and open to God interrupting your plan or taking you in a different direction than you envisioned. This is what it means to be a follower of Jesus Christ instead of merely making your own plans and asking God to bless them. God gave you abilities and interests for *His* purposes. You will find meaning and lasting purpose in the abilities God has given you only as they are presented back to Him for His use. When you do that, your life may take a detour or a different path altogether, and it may not always be fun. If you persist in submitting your life wholly to God no matter what happens, however, in time various elements of your life will blossom like a well-watered garden.

So make your plans and set your goals. That is good, so long as your goals are God-centered and not self-centered. But just know ahead of time that God, as your Maker and Father, has the right to tweak those plans for the purpose of His will in creating you. Don't be discouraged if your goals don't unfold exactly like how you would like or in your timing. If you work toward something of significance and meaning and have a plan for how to accomplish whatever God has set on your heart, it *will* happen in His timing and according to His direction for your life. And my experience has been that God will often shape the character and patience of His people by allowing them to flex their muscles of perseverance, which means that God's plans for you almost always take longer to unfold than you would like. Quitters don't see the end result of what God is doing, while those who persevere and continue to work toward their goals, regardless of the setbacks, do.

Many wonderful books and articles have been written that provide very detailed suggestions on how to goal-set effectively, and I recommend looking into some of these materials. Of note, the book, *Goals*, by Brian Tracy, and the previously-mentioned book by Steven Scott, *The Richest Man Who Ever Lived: King Solomon's Secrets to Success, Wealth, and Happiness*, are great resources on how to maximize goal setting.

On a closing note, according to a study done by Gail Matthews at Dominican University, those who wrote down their goals accomplished significantly more than those who did not write down their goals. This is actually only one study out of many showing the same. Additionally, research also shows that those who not only write down their goals but who look at them at least once a week are almost always more successful than those who write down their goals but then tuck them away and never look at them.

To further demonstrate the importance of writing down your goals and reviewing them often, consider research conducted by Virginia Tech University, which found that people who wrote down their goals (visions) earned NINE TIMES as much as those who did not write their goals. When asked, "What are your goals for life," the research revealed that:

- Eighty percent said they didn't know.
- Fifteen percent said they have goals but they've never written them down.
- Only 4% said they've written the goals, but have never gone back to look at them
- One percent said they wrote their goals and they review them on a weekly basis.

The researchers were diligent to point out that the one percent who wrote down their goals and reviewed them weekly were... MILLIONAIRES!

"Write the vision, and make it plain upon tablets, that he may run that readeth it."
   -Habakkuk 2:2 (KJV)

"Where there is no vision, the people perish: but he that keepeth the law, happy is he."
   -Proverbs 29:18 (KJV)

"Everybody has their own Mount Everest they were put on this earth to climb."
   -Seth Godin

"The first step toward creating an improved future is developing the ability to envision it. VISION will ignite the fire of passion that fuels our commitment to do WHATEVER IT TAKES to achieve excellence. Only VISION allows us to transform dreams of greatness into the reality of achievement through human action. VISION has no boundaries and knows no limits. Our VISION is what we become in life."
   -Tony Dungy

"A goal properly set is halfway reached."
   –Zig Ziglar

"All who have accomplished great things have had a great aim, have fixed their gaze on a goal which was high, one which sometimes seemed impossible."
   -Orison Swett Marden

"Give me a stock clerk with a goal and I'll give you a man who will make history. Give me a man with no goals and I'll give you a stock clerk."
   -J.C. Penney

25

An Overlooked Part of Success

Fred Astaire, the famous actor, dancer, and singer who rose to Hollywood fame in the 1930s, was without a doubt one of the top performers of his time. Beginning with his stage performances, which began in 1917, his career spanned a total of 76 years, during which he made 31 musical films and several television specials and musical recordings. He is best remembered as a flawless and rhythmic dancer, skills that he used to high-step into people's hearts in his series of Hollywood musicals. Astaire was ranked by the American Film as the fifth greatest male star of Classic Hollywood cinema in the ranking of 100 stars in 100 years.

Astaire's career, however, was not one that skyrocketed overnight or without significant challenges. When Astaire was attempting to make the transition from stage to film, a Hollywood talent judge wrote the following description of him after his screen test: "Can't act. Can't sing. Can dance a little." In spite of a rocky start in Hollywood, however, Astaire didn't let the initial failures deter him. He continued to work his craft and try and try again. The rest is history.

As Christians, we may fail badly at times, and perhaps often as we learn to put off the "old man" and put on the new. After disappointing lapses in judgment or character, we may think to ourselves, "What kind of Christian does that? How can I do anything significant for God after this?"

It is important to understand that as Christians we may have rocky starts ourselves, just as the disciple Peter did when he initially denied even knowing the Savior when he thought that denial would save his neck. Yet Peter went on to become one of the principle figures in the early Church. He became very familiar with the grace of God, which not only provided the means for second chances (and third, and fourth, and so on), but Peter also knew the strength that the grace of God provides in overcoming the baggage of personal failures and insecurities.

I identify with Peter. I can't tell you how many times I have failed in becoming the man I know God has called me to be. But I don't give up just because I blow it sometimes. I get back up, try to learn from my mistakes, and keep forging ahead. Even if I fail 10,000 times in the same area, I have not ultimately failed as long as I have breath in my body. God's mercies are new every morning and His lovingkindness is fresh each day (see Lamentations 3:22-23). If you have enough spiritual sensitivity to be disappointed by your sins and character flaws rather than trying to justify them and deflect responsibility, then that's a good sign. Don't be concerned about what happened yesterday or even the last ten years. Today is a new day. Learn from your mistakes, make the necessary adjustments, and go for it again. God is pleased with that kind of tenacity.

The principle of failure being an ingredient of success is also true beyond just one's Christian character. Whether in business, ministry, entertainment, or just life in general, people who have experienced significant levels of success almost never get there without first experiencing crushing failure, often several times. It is said of the great inventor, Thomas Edison, that he failed hundreds of times in attempting to refine the light bulb. With each failure, he would say that he just discovered one more way that it couldn't be done. In response to a New York Times reporter's question, Edison replied, "I have not failed 700 times. I have not failed once. I have succeeded in proving that those 700 ways will not work. When I have eliminated the ways that will not work, I will find the way that will work."

Edison's perspective on failure as being a prerequisite to success and his tenacious perseverance made him one of the greatest inventors in history.

As Thomas Edison, Fred Astaire, and the Apostle Peter demonstrated, a person never ultimately fails unless they simply give up. If a person does not understand that failure – and sometimes repeated failure – is part of the recipe for ultimate success, then he or she is more likely to give up at the first or second failure, or when the path to success is too bumpy and too many obstacles are in the way.

People fail in marriage and friendships because they did not understand from the beginning that successful relationships take work, and that sometimes there will be failures in the form of times of unrest or unhappiness, and it is in those times that one must learn and grow. If a person is unwilling to learn and grow, then ultimate and permanent failure awaits.

This is actually a very simple and basic concept, but one that most people have never been taught and few understand. Many young people come out of high school or college with visions of grandeur but without the gritty determination to withstand the onslaught of delays, failures, disappointments, and setbacks. And because people are afraid of failure, they will often never do anything even slightly risky for fear of losing something or embarrassing themselves. It's never fun to lose, but calculated risks are also part of the recipe for success. As the saying goes, "Nothing ventured [risked], nothing gained."

I believe that setbacks and failures are part of the success recipe because they help us to appreciate success when it comes. It also builds within us the work ethic and perseverance it takes to withstand disappointments and forge ahead anyway.

Remember also that failure is an opportunity to reinvent one's self. I read a short biography of actor Duane "The Rock" Johnson recently, who started out as a college football player and was aspiring to make it in the pros. His dream ended, however, with a back injury that halted his career. His dream of being in the NFL was done. But *he* wasn't. Rather than wallowing in the misery of his failed dream, he simply reinvented himself. He became a pro wrestler, and from there on to Hollywood fame as a very successful actor.

So don't be afraid of failure. If you fall flat on your face, simply get back up and keep marching. Whether in business, relationships, developing a new skill, or simply developing godly character, you'll get there eventually if you don't give up.

"The godly may trip seven times, but they will get up again. But one disaster is enough to overthrow the wicked."
    -Proverbs 24:16 (NLT)

"So do not throw away your confidence; it will be richly rewarded. You need to persevere so that when you have done the will of God, you will receive what he has promised. For...'I take no pleasure in the one who shrinks back'."
    -Hebrews 10:35-38 (NIV)

"No human ever became interesting by not failing. The more you fail and recover and improve, the better you are as a person. Ever meet someone who's always had everything work out for them with zero struggle? They usually have the depth of a puddle. Or they don't exist."
    - Chris Hardwick

"Pain is temporary. Quitting lasts forever."
- Lance Armstrong

"Failure should be our teacher, not our undertaker. Failure is delay, not defeat. It is a temporary detour, not a dead end. Failure is something we can avoid only by saying nothing, doing nothing, and being nothing."
- Denis Waitley

"Success is stumbling from failure to failure with no loss of enthusiasm."
- Winston Churchill

"Every adversity, every failure, every heartache carries with it the seed of an equal or greater benefit."
- Napoleon Hill

"Everything you want is on the other side of fear."
- Jack Canfield

"Only those who dare to fail greatly can ever achieve greatly."
- Robert F. Kennedy

"Many a brilliant man with drive, pep, enthusiasm, personality, and seemingly all the qualities of leadership has yet failed because he let some obstacle or series of obstacles stop him dead."
-R.G. LeTourneau

26

Vinegar to the Teeth and Smoke to the Eyes

"Like vinegar to the teeth and smoke to the eyes, so the slacker is to the one who sends him on an errand."
-Proverbs 10:26 (HCSB)

There is perhaps no other person so frustrating to friends, family, and work associates as the one on whom they cannot depend. People who are habitually late, who do not follow through with their commitments, and who bail out on responsibilities are those who will find themselves eventually under-employed or unemployed, and with a pretty small list of good friends.

While an unreliable person is a frustration to others, ultimately they are a frustration to themselves and might not even realize it. Unreliable people are usually not asked to be involved in anything important. Whether in the workplace, in church, or even social events, the most that an unreliable person might be called on to do is to help clean up afterward, because people might be able to depend on that person to at least be there for the *end* of the event. Therefore, unreliable people do not progress in the workplace, in the social pecking order, or in ministry to any significant degree. They are the people others make jokes about when not in earshot.

Of course, it is not possible to be 100% reliable for everything because sometimes life does get in the way. People get sick unexpectedly, tires go flat without warning, cars break down on the worst possible day, etc. Things happen. We all realize that and can be gracious to others when unexpected crisis occur. But good excuses will take you only so far when you seem to have "good" excuses repeatedly. If that happens often enough, no one is going to buy your good excuse anymore, and they will write you off as someone on whom they cannot depend.

If life happens and something unexpected gets in the way, here's what to do:

As soon as humanly possible, call the people who are relying on you and explain the situation and ask to be excused. If it's possible to find a replacement, do it yourself. Don't put extra strain on the people who are relying on you to find that replacement when you might be able to do it. Go the extra mile in trying to make the inconvenience of you not being able to follow through as easy on others as possible.

There is a saying that goes like this: "If you want something done right, give it to a busy person." That might sound counterintuitive, but the logic is sound. If a person is busy, it usually (not always) means he or she is busy because lots of people rely on him or her. That person has a reputation of getting a job or project done excellently and on time. If, on the other hand, a person finds himself or herself without much to do, it might mean that people have learned to not give that person any project of importance because of either not following through, or being late in getting things done, or doing a shoddy job.

Reliability is, unfortunately, not high on the priority list of a growing number of people in today's society because of laziness, entitlement, or both. Therefore, someone who is a Mr. or Ms. Reliability will stand out in a good way.

Some ways to help you become more reliable are:

1. Have a do-it-now mentality. Don't procrastinate. Don't put off until later what you can do right now. Get it out of the way.

2. Plan your tasks in order of importance, and/or do your least enjoyable tasks first to get them marked off your list. Many people put off their least enjoyable tasks until last, but sometimes the least enjoyable tasks are the most important ones. Get the most important tasks out of the way first so that you know they get done, and get done excellently. Don't end up being rushed and then cut corners with your most important tasks.

3. Write down your to-do list as tasks come up. Don't rely on your memory. Your memory will sometimes let you down, especially if you are very busy and hurried.

As a last thought on this point, it must also be understood by the reliable person that reliable people like yourself are not very plentiful. Reliable people can be very frustrated by the number of unreliable people in the world. At the end of the day, you have to know in advance that people are going to let you down and fail to live up to your expectations. If you are a boss or someone in a position of authority, this is where clear communication of your expectations is necessary.

I strive to be a reliable person myself, and during my years as a worship leader I often made the mistake of expecting people to have the same commitments to excellence, moral integrity, and reliability as me. Since I, as a 30-something young man at the time, already knew some of these principles, I took it for granted that others knew these principles, too. Boy, was I wrong! I was shocked by how little people knew in this area. So the very first book I ever wrote, *The Complete Worship Ministry Handbook*, was directed to worship team members to help them understand what was expected of them in ministry.

Even with clearly communicated expectations and standards in place, however, people will still find a way to let you down.

You just have to fix it in your mind that the only person on whom you can rely 100% of the time is God, because, really, you can't even rely on yourself 100% of the time. All of us would have to admit that there are times when we did not follow through with our own commitment to ourselves. Whether it's losing weight or whatever the commitment to yourself is, we have all blown it. We tend to be very generous with mercy on ourselves when we fail, but reliable people do have the weakness of being harder on others than they should, perhaps. While we certainly should not entrust important assignments to people who have not shown trustworthiness, at the same time we should extend grace when people do blow it and disappoint us. We will walk through life rubbing shoulders with unreliable people all our days. Thus, a balance of clear communication, high standards, and mercy should be the order of the day.

"Like a snow-cooled drink at harvest time is a trustworthy messenger to the one who sends him; he refreshes the spirit of his master."
-**Proverbs 25:13** (NIV)

"Trusting a fool to convey a message is like cutting off one's feet or drinking poison!"
-**Proverbs 26:6** (NLT)

"You need not wonder if you should have an unreliable person as a friend. An unreliable person is no one's friend."
-**Idries Shah**

27

Be Hearty in Your Approbation

Charles Schwab, the American steel tycoon in the early 1900s who went on to become a success guru of sorts, is famous for saying, "Be hearty in your approbation and lavish in your praise." Schwab knew how to win with people, and that was part of his recipe for his extraordinary success.

One of Schwab's ingredients in his success recipe was how to win the hearts of people and make everyone, even his employees, feel like they were his friends and were important to him. This involved finding something about which to praise people and being lavish in that praise.

Empty flattery, mind you, is not what I am referring to here. Schwab found something he genuinely appreciated or admired in someone, and then he was hearty in his approbation. And everyone loved him for it.

Too many people are very liberal with criticism but tight-lipped when it comes to compliments or appreciation. This order is backwards. We should endeavor to be restrained with criticisms but generous with expressing appreciation. When you express genuine appreciation for someone, you feed their hungry souls. Mark Twain once said, "I can live for a month on a good compliment."

Think about it. What does it do for you when someone is hearty in their praise of you? If nurtures you, doesn't it? Isn't it true that we are all insecure at some level? Heartfelt compliments make us feel like we really matter, like we truly have something significant to contribute to the world.

I am convinced that one of the greatest scourges of mankind is starvation. Not just starvation from food, although that is a terrible plight as well. Starvation of appreciation is a worldwide epidemic. People are starving for significance, for love, and for someone to admire or appreciate them. This is why people often react so severely to the smallest criticism, but will open up to you like a blossoming flower in the morning sun when you appreciate them.

A sure-fire way to overcome the awkwardness of meeting new people, especially if you are the shy type, is simply to find something to compliment them on, like part of their apparel perhaps, and then watch them warm up to you. You can keep the conversation flowing by simply asking them some questions about themselves, and then show genuine interest in their career or hobbies and compliment them for their expertise in that area.

Recently I was in a social setting where a gentleman was showing me his favorite hobby and displaying some of the things he and his family built together. Now, I honestly wasn't the slightest bit interested in his hobby. But I was trying to show interest in *him*, so I let him talk and listened for things with which I might be genuinely impressed. And indeed, after listening to his technical jargon for a few minutes I realized what a truly creative and intelligent person this man is. So I complimented him on his extraordinary skills and praised him for his creativity. And this man, although sharing nothing in common with me and is probably not the slightest bit interested in the things that interest me, nevertheless seems to genuinely like me simply because I took a few moments to feed his ego and self-image. It's such an easy thing to do, but so few people do it because they are always looking for their own ways to impress people.

It's true that starving people will rarely go out of their way to feed someone else. And this is certainly true with people who are emotionally starving. They are so desperate to feed their own self-esteem that they forget that there are millions of other emotionally starving people out there, too. But God has created the world in a most interesting way by building into our universe something called the Law of Sowing and Reaping. When you feed others, life will see to it that you get fed as well. Whether physical food or food for your soul, when you give, you receive.

Those who are hearty in their approbation and lavish in their praise are usually the most secure and happy people on the planet. But those who are stingy with compliments are generally unhappy and tend to stay that way because their focus is always on themselves.

"Anxiety in a man's heart weighs it down, but a good word makes it glad."
-Proverbs 12:25 (ESV)

"Everyone enjoys a fitting reply; it is wonderful to say the right thing at the right time!"
-Proverbs 15:23 (NLT)

"When someone who loves and cares about me compliments me, I feel more glamorous than when the flashbulbs are going off on the red carpet."
-Gabrielle Union

"It's easy to pay someone a compliment when you arrive at the place of emotional security where you are no longer starving for them yourself."
–Yours Truly

28

Rejoice with Those Who Rejoice, Weep with Those Who Weep

The title of this chapter is taken word-for-word from Romans 12:15. It speaks of an important social grace to be supportive of others in good times and in bad, and to know what is appropriate for any given situation.

I politely offered that perspective to a person who was cracking jokes and laughing loudly during a post-funeral dinner. The deceased had died unexpectedly, and many people present were, of course, grieving. When the person encouraged me to lighten up after I did not laugh at the ill-timed jokes, I responded, "This isn't the time." The reply was, "[The deceased] would want us to be happy." That was true, of course, but the people around us may have felt the sting of ill-timed humor during their grieving. It wasn't about the deceased. It was about those who were weeping. And in order to show them proper respect and support, we should have been "weeping" with them, or at least not acting like we were at a party.

While it is just proper etiquette to be sympathetic to those who weep, it is equally important to rejoice with those who rejoice.

Many years ago my wife, Donna, and I were blessed to have

built and owned our first home. It wasn't extravagant by most standards, but it was a huge step forward for us, and we were delighted with it. A couple we knew well came over to visit, and of course we were eager to share our joy with them. The husband obeyed Charles Schwab's mandate. He was "hearty in his approbation and lavish with his praise." He oohed and aahed over many features of the house. The wife, on the other hand, said barely a word. She walked through the house numbly and without emotion. It almost seemed as if the little five-minute tour was annoying or boring to her. When the couple left, we loved the husband more than we ever had, but the wife had made a major withdrawal on the balance of her brownie points. Perhaps she felt jealous. Maybe our house represented something she wanted but did not yet have. She and her husband had a nice house, but it was rented at the time. I understand that success should not be rubbed in the noses of people, and that's a social grace, too. But this couple was close to us at the time, and we felt we could share our joy with them and that they would celebrate with us. But the wife refused to, and it left us with a very negative feeling about her.

Perhaps we were too enthusiastic with the joy of our new home, granted. Over the years, I have learned to downplay whatever success I have enjoyed because of the fact that some people react negatively to people who do better than they do. Nevertheless, it is always wise to share other people's joys and successes even if it seems to shine the spotlight on your own shortcomings. No one likes a Negative Nellie, especially when the negativity seems to be aimed directly at you or your blessings. Even if you have to do it through gritted teeth, rejoice with those who rejoice, and you will add points to the emotional love bank of the people with whom you rejoice.

And it's just good manners.

"Like one who takes away a garment on a cold day, or like vinegar poured on a wound, is one who sings songs to a heavy heart."
-**Proverbs 25:20** (NIV)

"Rejoicing in the good fortune of others is a practice that can help us when we feel emotionally shut down and unable to connect with others. Rejoicing generates good will."
-**Pema Chodron**

"He who fears to weep, should learn to be kind to those who weep."
-**Abu Bakr**

29

Give a Tenth, Save a Tenth

It is said that the number one issue that married couples fight over is money. Money problems can put terrible stress on the body and emotions and put a dark cloud over one's life. Learning to wisely manage your financial household is a very important principle in learning how to be good at life.

The best thing you can do for your financial estate is to live off 80% of your income or less. It is a fundamental financial principle of both secular economics and Biblical economics to get in the habit of giving and saving. If you get in this habit when you are young, things will go much better for you in life as you progress in your career and income.

Most people spend close to 100% of their income, and debt allows them to spend even more than 100%, at least for a while.

Some economists might suggest to live off 70% of your income, and the other 30% should be divided up into 10% giving, 10% savings, and 10% investing. The Bible also teaches all three principles.

The back half of Proverbs 31 is the famous section on what has become known as "the wife of noble character." One of the qualities of the Proverbs 31 woman is her ability to manage well the financial estate of the house by investing and doing business as a sidebar to her other household responsibilities. The larger part of the financial sections of Proverbs, however, have to do with the other two principles of giving and saving.

Some miserly people are great at saving and heaping up unto themselves but rarely, if ever, give. This is called stinginess. Others feel that it is their spiritual obligation to live on barely anything and give away practically everything. But the Bible teaches the virtue of saving money as a principle equal to that of giving as long as the saving does not become stinginess. Both are important.

Since the benefits of saving and good money management are self-evident, I will not elaborate on those points here, but will instead focus my attention on the benefits of giving, since giving money away does not seem like something that is personally beneficial. Indeed, giving represents a mysterious paradox.

Let me state clearly that both the Bible and secular economists promote generosity not only because of how it benefits mankind, but also for how it benefits the giver. For example, author and financial adviser, David Bach, has written six consecutive national bestsellers on managing money and growing wealth. His book, *The Automatic Millionaire,* was a runaway bestseller when it was first published in 2004, and it spent fourteen weeks on the New York Times bestseller list. In that book, Bach devotes an entire chapter to what he calls tithing, which he describes as giving *at least ten percent* of your income to non-profit organizations like a church or ministry. To my knowledge, David Bach is not a Christian. But the reason he stresses giving at least ten percent of one's income so heavily is because he has discovered and freely acknowledges that, somehow, money is attracted to those who give.

He writes,

> *"Although you should give simply for the sake of giving, the reality is that abundance tends to flow back to those who give. The more you give, the more comes back to you. It is the flow of abundance that*

brings us more joy, more love, more wealth, and more meaning in our lives. Generally speaking, the more you give, the wealthier you feel. And it's not just a feeling. As strange as it may seem, the truth is that money often flows faster to those who give. Why? Because givers attract abundance into their lives rather than scarcity."

The Bible, of course, was the original document that spoke of the paradox of giving.

"One person gives freely, yet gains even more; another withholds unduly, but comes to poverty. A generous person will prosper; whoever refreshes others will be refreshed."
-Proverbs 11:24-25 (NIV)

This is only one of dozens of exhortations and examples of generosity throughout Scripture. From Genesis through the New Testament, generosity in many forms is not only encouraged, but commanded.

The starting point of generosity in scripture is with the "tithe," which means *tenth*, and by implication means the first ten percent off the top and always goes to your local house of worship. You should arrange your financial budget around the tithe, budgeting everything else around that. If there is anything left over after your expenditures and savings, you should also make an effort to give alms to the poor and participate in special offerings at times, all of which are represented in scripture.

The concept of tithing has come under fire in recent years by certain groups who claim that tithing was reserved for Old Testament law and was lifted under the New Covenant. I do not have the room in this short chapter to address those issues, but I have written an entire book on the subject that is a thorough examination of both the Old and New Testaments on the subject of tithing. It demonstrates that tithing is a moral principle that preceded the Levitical Law and is therefore timeless. If you wish to study this out more, my book, *Tithing in the New Testament Age: Is it Biblical?*, might be a good place to begin. In fact, reading up to only chapter 2 will probably resolve the issue for you if you have questions about tithing. You can find my book on my ministry website at AndrewRobbinsMinistries.org.

In that book and my earlier work, *The Pillars of Prosperity*, I share the testimony of how my wife and I started our marriage in a very difficult place financially and I did not have the education or skill to expect to make it very far in the corporate world. The secret to the success that my wife and I have enjoyed is not because we are especially talented or skilled in the world of business. We have grown in knowledge and skill in a few areas over the years, but we didn't start out that way. I was a long-haired musician wannabee who knew nothing of making it in the world of business. Because we have honored God with our money and have been firmly committed to tithing and other acts of generosity, we have enjoyed God's favor. I am absolutely convinced that my entrance into the corporate world was because of God's divine placement, and from that starting place God has continued to bless us.

So fall in love with giving and being a blessing, and God will get involved with your finances.

Giving is only part of the equation of living without financial pressure, however. As already stated, one must learn to save and wisely manage his financial affairs. Wisely managing one's financial estate is a topic too long to address in this format, but books and courses abound on this subject. If you are not sure how to wisely manage your financial affairs, educate yourself. You might begin with the late Larry Burkett's work with Crown Financial Ministries at Crown.org.

"Give, and it will be given to you. A good measure, pressed down, shaken together and running over, will be poured into your lap. For with the measure you use [to give], it will be measured [back] to you."
-Luke 6:38 (NIV)

"⁶Remember this: Whoever sows sparingly will also reap sparingly, and whoever sows generously will also reap generously. ⁷Each man should give what he has decided in his heart to give, not reluctantly or under compulsion, for God loves a cheerful giver. ⁸And God is able to make all grace abound to you, so that in all things at all times, having all that you need, you will abound in every good work. ⁹As it is written: 'He has scattered abroad his gifts to the poor; his righteousness endures for ever.' ¹⁰Now he who supplies seed to the sower and bread for food will also supply and increase your store of seed and will enlarge the harvest of your righteousness. ¹¹You will be enriched in every way so that you can be generous on every occasion, and through us your generosity will result in thanksgiving to God."
-2 Corinthians 9:6-15 (NIV)

"Not he who has much is rich, but he who gives much."
-Erich Fromm

"Money is like love; it kills slowly and painfully the one who withholds it, and enlivens the other who turns it on his fellow man."
-Kahlil Gibran

"If you would be wealthy, think of saving as well as getting."
   -Benjamin Franklin

"Beware of little expenses. A small leak will sink a great ship."
   -Benjamin Franklin

"There are plenty of ways to get ahead. The first is so basic I'm almost embarrassed to say it: spend less than you earn."
   - Paul Clitheroe

30

The Importance of Forgiveness

As we have now looked at 29 principles in learning to be good at life, let's get one thing clear: you are not perfect and will never master all of these principles perfectly all the time. You are human and you will make mistakes. As James 3:2 says, we all stumble in many ways. So just as you need to be watchful against pride, equally important is the potential landmine of self-loathing and unforgiveness toward one's self. When you make mistakes, even big ones, you must forgive yourself, learn from it, and move on.

While forgiving yourself is an observation to keep in mind, the primary point of this chapter is the importance of forgiveness toward others. Most people do not suffer from self-loathing. That is definitely something that a small portion of our society may deal with, but the larger part deals with the problem of exonerating ourselves for our mistakes but pounding the gavel of judgment toward others, and that is especially true when the actions of others affect you personally in a negative way.

If you want to be good at life and be well thought of, you will have to learn to look past the mistakes, sins, and thoughtlessness of others. And when I say look past them, I certainly do not mean to imply that you have to put up with everything. There is a time to speak up, and there is a time to cut off some toxic relationships.

But by and large, each of us should endeavor to exercise the same mercy that we want extended to us. If we want mercy, we must extend mercy.

Mercy is not always easy. Mercy means you will have to muzzle your mouth and not respond the way your emotions want you to respond. Mercy means you may have to "lose" some arguments and refrain from cutting offenders down a few sizes when you know you could verbally dominate them if you choose. Mercy means leaving the judging in the hands of the One Who is Judge over all and Who knows the hearts of each person.

One of the best examples of a merciful person I know is my longtime friend and former pastor, Tracy McIntyre. Tracy has always been very good with people, very unlike me in my earlier years. He still exceeds me in that respect by light years, even though I feel I have grown in that area a lot. I have known Tracy since I was 16 and he was 20. I can look back now and remember many knuckleheaded things I have said and many stupid and careless things I have done that Tracy witnessed. A few times those foolish things affected him personally. But not once have I ever felt judged by him. Never has he made me feel like I was stupid or thoughtless. Even the rare times he has responded at all to something reckless I said, it wasn't in a judgmental way. He has always been very good at making light of awkward situations while simultaneously and skillfully making me aware that he noticed a less-than-courteous comment launched in his direction. Whenever I remember something like that, I cringe at myself, of course, but my positive feelings about Tracy's character is strengthened. I want to be like Tracy when I grow up!

It would have been so easy for Tracy to have taken me to task in the past and to make a point of cutting me down a few notches. And he probably would have been justified in some of those situations. But then what? Would that have made me gain respect for him? Not likely. Especially in my earlier years, a harsh rebuke would have likely made me resent him, and most people are exactly the same way. Tracy's policy has been to lead by example, to address problems with people in only the most extreme situations, and to live a life of forgiveness and mercy. And what an example he is because of those personal practices. Without saying a word of rebuke to me, Tracy has been one of the best teachers I have ever had simply because I have watched his life and learned from him.

On the other hand, forgiving small foibles is one thing. But what about the people who may wound you or wrong you in terrible ways? Do we have to forgive them, too?

I read a saying once that went like this: "Bitterness is like drinking poison and hoping the other person will die." When you are bitter toward someone, it harms only you, not the offender. Medical research has proven that strong, unresolved negative emotions tend to be very hard on one's physical and emotional health. Bitterness and unresolved anger initiate the release of stress hormones and alarm chemicals throughout the body that can be very destructive to the brain, nervous system, heart, and tissues. That's why Proverbs 14:30 says,

> **"A tranquil heart is life to the body, but passion is rottenness to the bones."** (NLT)

The Hebrew word for "passion" there is *qinah*, the larger meaning of which refers to anger, envy, jealousy, rivalry, and zeal. It has to do with deep unresolved toxic emotions. And those unresolved emotions are as "rottenness to the bones." In other words, they are noxious to your body, your mind, and your soul. You cannot have a tranquil heart as long as you are harboring *qinah* emotions.

Every person I have ever met who harbors resentment and anger toward someone is a person in whom I can easily spot unrest. I have been one of those people, so I speak from experience. There is no peace for the person who harbors unforgiveness. Even during times of relaxation and fun, bitter people are never truly at peace, not deep down. That bitterness eats at them, and it tends to have an effect on how that person responds to other people and how they view life. The saying is true, "hurting people hurt people." Hurting people will first hurt themselves with their own bitterness toward someone else, and then they will inevitably torpedo other relationships along the way, always blaming the other person, and heaping up offense after offense that they harbor in their hearts.

This, I believe, is part of what Jesus meant when He said in Matthew 18:34 that the person who has been forgiven much but nevertheless refuses to forgive the offenses of others will be "delivered over to the tormentors" (KJV). Jesus was, of course, using a parable as a teaching illustration that has been referred to as the parable of the unmerciful servant. The tormentors in the parable were the jailers, and everything in the parable represents something in real life. The master represents God; the unmerciful servant represents you and me; the fellow servants represents everyone else with whom we come into contact and who many offend us from time to time; and the jailers could represent demons or any other kind of mental or emotional torment. When we refuse to forgive, we open ourselves up to demonic torment that can manifest in terrible physical, emotional, relational, mental, and spiritual problems. I have seen that very thing more times than I care to count.

A Nearly-Extinct Virtue

On this point about forgiveness, let's revisit an earlier point about loyalty, since the two are related.

Loyalty is defined as a strong sense of support or allegiance. It means sticking by someone through thick and thin even when they are a little rough around the edges at times. Too many people in our society have no concept of what it means to be loyal to a spouse, a friend, a church and pastor, or a boss and company. They run out on people so easily when they get offended over something petty or when it seems to immediately benefit them.

And that impedes progress in business, ministry, and meaningful relationships.

In Ben Sira, one of the apocryphal books that appears only in Catholic Bibles, in verse 9, it says, *"Do not abandon old friends, for new ones cannot equal them."* Proverbs 17:17 follows suit: *"A friend loves at all times, and a brother is born for a time of adversity."* That means that a true friend loves you during good times and bad, when you are at your best or your worst, when you agree and disagree, and when you are at odds. It means that a true friend will demonstrate the depth of that friendship by being supportive and loyal during times of adversity, and will not allow petty differences to divide your relationship. A friend who easily abandons you during time of adversity or differences was never your true friend to begin with. He was a fair-weather friend.

If you want to be a desirable person, someone who others look to and admire, then make forgiveness and loyalty your trademarks.

"Do not judge, and you will not be judged. Do not condemn, and you will not be condemned. Forgive, and you will be forgiven."
-Luke 6:37 (NIV)

"He has shown you, O mortal, what is good. And what does the LORD require of you? To act justly and to love mercy and to walk humbly with your God."
-Micah 6:8 (NIV)

"To be a Christian means to forgive the inexcusable because God has forgiven the inexcusable in you."
-C.S. Lewis

"We have to recognize that there cannot be relationships unless there is commitment, unless there is loyalty, unless there is love, patience, persistence."

-Cornel West

31

The Greatest Commandments

Here we are at the last pointer in being good at life. I'm glad you stuck around this long.

I want to begin this chapter by saying that while the principles we have discussed so far are specific in nature, there is one overarching theme into which all of these principles can be distilled. It is found in the words of Jesus.

> [29]*"The most important is this...*[30]*Love the Lord your God with all your heart and with all your soul and with all your mind and with all your strength.* [31]*The second is this: 'Love your neighbor as yourself.' There is no commandment greater than these."*
> *-Mark 12:30-31* (NIV)

> *"So in everything, do to others what you would have them do to you, for this sums up the Law and the Prophets."*
> *-Luke 7:12* (NIV)

If you endeavor to truly love the Lord with all your soul, mind, and strength, and to love your neighbor as yourself, treating people the way you would want to be treated, many of the principles discussed in this book will fall into place naturally and eventually become second-nature to you.

Thus, many of these principles are simply heart issues. In other words, what is truly in your heart will naturally manifest outwardly. If you are a self-centered and prideful person, that is going to become evident to the people around you. If you are a selfless, caring, and humble person, that, too, is going to be evident to the people around you. You may be able to fake it for a while, but a leopard cannot change its spots, as the saying goes. You cannot change what is in your heart, and it will manifest no matter how hard you try.

A person cannot change what is in his or her heart just by trying to be a better person. You can change some things outwardly and perhaps begin being more generous and dispensing with demeaning humor in favor of more gracious speech, etc. Identifying wrong behavior and correcting it is good, and people can do so with *some* behaviors just as a matter of choice. But there are other things they cannot change and will never change without a transformation of the heart and mind.

But how do you get there? How does a person get to the place of having a transformation of the heart and mind to the point where it consequently manifests outwardly into more honorable behavior? Well, let me state bluntly that it cannot occur without two things happening: 1) the Holy Spirit drawing you to God, and 2) you responding to that beckoning.

I was 26-years-old when I made a firm decision to truly follow Christ and give up my own life to be His disciple. I had been an angry, selfish, and immoral person prior to that decision. On that spring day in 1992 I knelt on a chair in my bedroom, repented and asked Jesus to take the driver's seat of my life. I emerged from that room with a new life and a new attitude toward myself and the world. A few things were immediately different as a result. Gone was my anger toward the world and my explosive, violent temper. I threw out my stash of pornography and cut off the immoral relationships I was having with multiple young ladies. My vile speech also just magically disappeared.

But there were a few other things I had to work through.

You see, when I made that decision to love God with all my heart, mind, soul, and strength, God got busy right away doing His transformative work in my life. But that transformative work also required my cooperation. God was faithful to show me that He was indeed now involved in my life by giving me a new heart that made me want to please Him. And while that new heart expressed itself immediately in some changes in character and behavior that I didn't even have to try to change, there were other things I needed to root out of my heart by seeking God diligently through prayer and repeated exposure to His written Word. The insecurity buried deep in my psyche didn't immediately vanish, for example. Neither did the tendencies toward selfishness and pride. Those things have been Achilles heels, weak points in my character that God has progressively showed me are there, and ridding myself of those corruptions has been a long and arduous process. I'm still not where I want to be, but I'm moving forward and making progress.

So yes, there are behaviors that you can and should change, and that's what this book has been about: correcting behaviors that have the ability to prevent you from having your best life. But a person can put on a good front and look good on the outside and still be full of pride, selfishness, and perversion on the inside. That's why Jesus was very hard on the religious teachers of his time because they were hypocrites. Jesus said to them,

> [25]"Woe to you, teachers of the law and Pharisees, you hypocrites! You clean the outside of the cup and dish, but inside they are full of greed and self-indulgence. [26]Blind Pharisee! First clean the inside of the cup and dish, and then the outside also will be clean. [27]Woe to you, teachers of the law and Pharisees, you hypocrites! You are like whitewashed

tombs, which look beautiful on the outside but on the inside are full of the bones of the dead and everything unclean. [28]In the same way, on the outside you appear to people as righteous but on the inside you are full of hypocrisy and wickedness."
  -*Matthew 23:25-28* (NIV)

Wow! Jesus didn't mince words when it came to hypocrisy, did He?

The point is that a person can polish up the outside, and that's good, in a way, to improve where you see the need. Without a change of heart, however, those outward improvements will never make you right with God, because God knows what is really in your heart much more than you do. That's why Jeremiah 17:9 says,

"The human heart is the most deceitful of all things, and desperately wicked. Who really knows how bad it is?" (NLT)

You see, the outward improvements must flow from an inner attitude. Many people try to change from the outside in, but it doesn't work that way. You have to change inwardly first, and then the outward change will come. That's why the Apostle John wrote,

"Beloved, I wish above all things that thou mayest prosper and be in health, even as thy soul prospereth."
  -*3 John 1:2* (KJV)

John was speaking of an outward expression of what was already going on inwardly. It was the hope of the Apostle John that the people of God would prosper inwardly, and as they did they would also prosper outwardly. And that is my hope with those who read this book.

As you have read through this book, I pray that one of the things that the study of these life principles has done for you is to shine a spotlight on some of the corruptions in your own heart, because we all have them. If there is unforgiveness, self-centeredness, or any other sinful tendency in your heart, I pray that studying these principles will help you to recognize them and deal with them through seeking God's presence and strength in your life.

Please understand that one of the reasons that God may eradicate some sinful tendencies when you decide to serve Him but leave others is so that we can learn just how corrupt at heart we all really are, and to seek Him earnestly as we endeavor to chisel our character into Christ-likeness. You can't root out the inner corruption of lust, for example, just by flipping a switch in your brain and deciding to not be lustful anymore. Believe me, I speak from experience. You have to seek God with all your heart and delight yourself in your relationship with Him, and as you do, you will renew your strength to fight the good fight of faith and change your character little by little.

> *"They who wait for the LORD shall renew their strength; they shall mount up with wings like eagles; they shall run and not be weary; they shall walk and not faint."*
> -Isaiah 40:31 (ESV)

The word for "wait" there in the ancient Hebrew is *qavah*, which also means *to eagerly look for*. When we eagerly pursue God, we will find the strength to do battle against our inner corruptions and win. You cannot change your own heart just by deciding to be good. You have to have a change of heart that comes only from the One Who knows your heart infinitely better than you do.

When you love God supremely and seek Him out through serious study of His Word, passionate prayer and fasting, heartfelt worship, and meeting together regularly with the saints and exposing yourself to good, challenging and insightful preaching and teaching, and when you see difficulties and trials as things that God can use as the refining process to expose our inner corruptions, remove the dross from the silver and cause us to seek Him even more diligently, then the wisdom of His ways and beauty of His character will become your own over time.

So if you find difficulty in changing your behavior and adopting some of the principles in this book, and if you are not experiencing the kind of speedy transformation that you had hoped for, don't despair. If you are seeking God, those things will come as long as you do not harden your heart. Change may come little by little at times through much failure and disappointment. But that's part of the process because you can learn great lessons and gain valuable insight from your failures that you can use both for your own benefit and for the benefit of others.

It is a privilege to pass along a little of the wisdom that I have learned from my own years of failures, disappointments, trials and successes walking with the LORD. I pray that in some way you were enriched as you have read through these principles. I will leave you now with the words of the prophets Micah and Jeremiah:

> *"He has shown you, O mortal, what is good. And what does the LORD require of you? To act justly and to love mercy and to walk humbly with your God."*
> *-Micah 6:8* (NIV)

> *"You will seek Me and find Me when you seek Me with all of your heart."*
> *-Jeremiah 29:13* (NIV)

Bonus Section

Planning for Your Final Destination

The previous chapters have been golden nuggets of wisdom geared toward living a better life, in some respects, than the one you have now. Even if the life you have right now is everything that you want it to be, you can continue growing and developing right up until the time you leave this earth – *if* you are open to continuing to learn that long, that is.

As I mentioned in the introduction, there is much more to learn about life and people than can be covered in one book. I encourage you to keep reading, seeking, learning, and growing. If you are wise, you will never feel that you have arrived in your personal development. The wisest and most accomplished people I know continue to feed their minds, bodies, and spirits right up through old age.

While the pursuit of wisdom is good, however, there is another perspective to consider. I will quote from the book of Ecclesiastes and then elaborate on my point.

> [12]*"Then I turned my thoughts to consider wisdom, and also madness and folly. What more can the king's successor do than what has already been done?* [13]*I saw that wisdom is better than folly,*

just as light is better than darkness. ¹⁴The wise have eyes in their heads, while the fool walks in the darkness; but I came to realize that the same fate overtakes them both. ¹⁵Then I said to myself, 'The fate of the fool will overtake me also. What then do I gain by being wise?' I said to myself, 'This too is meaningless.' ¹⁶For the wise, like the fool, will not be long remembered; the days have already come when both have been forgotten. Like the fool, the wise too must die!"

    -Ecclesiastes 2:12-16 (NIV)

The book of Ecclesiastes in the Bible is attributed to King Solomon, the wisest, most learned, and most successful man of his time. Toward the end of his life, he set pen to paper to reflect on his life and accomplishments, and to pass along what he had learned to succeeding generations. I find it interesting that this wise and powerful man, rich beyond imagination and renowned for his knowledge and wisdom, said in the latter years of his life that the pursuit of knowledge and wisdom is good in some respects, but in the final analysis, this too is meaningless and chasing after the wind because the wise and foolish both come to the same end, which is death.

If that was all of Ecclesiastes a person ever read, it would likely lead to the scratching of one's head in confusion. The preceding book of Proverbs, after all, which was also authored mostly by Solomon, is full of exhortations to pursue wisdom like your life depends on it. How could Solomon do an about-face and say that the pursuit of wisdom is folly?

Reading the Biblical books of Proverbs and Ecclesiastes in their entirety provides the answer to that question. Knowledge and wisdom can catapult a person's life from one of obscurity and futility to one of great accomplishment and purpose in this life. But what about the end of one's life? A fool and a sage both come to the same end, which is the grave. I know it's a morbid thought, perhaps, but the ultimate statistic is still true: *ten out of ten people die.*

Morbid or not, the truly wise consider more than just the short 70 or 80 years that we humans get the privilege of living out on this earth. The wise also consider the life after this life.

> **"It is better to go to a house of mourning than**
> **to go to a house of feasting, for death is the destiny**
> **of everyone; the living should take this to heart."**
> **-Ecclesiastes 7:2** (NIV)

The Most Important Planning You will Ever Do

In illustrating what I will lay out in this final section, let me paint a scenario for you. Let's imagine that you want to plan a vacation with your family. Let's imagine that you live in Wyoming and your vacation destination will be somewhere in Florida. Where in Florida, you don't yet know. You just want to go to Florida. So for weeks, you meticulously plan your travel schedule by RV through the highways and byways between Wyoming and Florida, a long drive, no doubt. You look up all the rest stops along the way on the internet, the camp sites, the site-seeing attractions on the route, and the restaurants and hotels. Everything is planned out perfectly. You have used your experience in planning the trip very well. You are knowledgeable in this area, and that knowledge will be used to your advantage as you travel.

Let's also imagine that your long journey has gone just as you planned, but you got so busy mapping out the trip that you forgot to actually plan for the exact destination. Imagine the futility of planning your trip so meticulously but then realizing as you cross the state line into Florida that you have no particular destination in mind, no resort reservations, and no money left to stay anywhere because you hadn't actually planned that far ahead.

Well, at this point you are probably saying to yourself that no one would be that stupid. Wrong! People do it all the time in the form of planning only for this life and not their final destination.

There is one line in the Bible that speaks of this destination; a phrase very short in length but very forceful in power, much like a boxer's jab.

> *"...each person is destined to die once and after*
> *that comes judgment..."*
> **-Hebrews 9:27** (BSB)

Very unlike the notion of reincarnation, the Bible teaches that each person is given one chance at life, and afterward life goes on in another dimension – the spiritual dimension; and it is here that the Great Judge of the Universe will examine each life lived on earth. It is this fact that I would be remiss to not address in a book about being good at life, because a life well lived is one that plans for the future.

Are there Many Ways to God, and How can a Person Know they are Right with God?

I am an analytical person. I have worked in a research-based science field for more than two decades and I enjoy the process of investigation. One thing I have learned about science and research is that the researcher must set aside all personal biases and opinions and simply go where the evidence leads. Of course, these rules have been suspended in some cases where scientific fraud is now not uncommon, unfortunately, but that's a point not germane to this discussion. My point is that it would be irresponsible to try to come to any conclusion about any matter based simply on hearsay, opinions, tradition, personal experience, or incomplete data. Yet this is exactly how some people arrive at their opinions about God, eternity, and spiritual matters in many, if not most cases.

I have heard it said that some people climb the ladder of success only to find out at the end of their lives that the ladder is leaning against the wrong wall! What a horrific thing it would be to believe all your life that you are doing good with your life and on good terms with God only to find out after it's too late and that you had been deceived. Some may roll their eyes at this suggestion, but Jesus addressed that very thing when He said,

> ²¹"Not everyone who says to me, 'Lord, Lord,' will enter the kingdom of heaven, but only the one who does the will of my Father who is in heaven. ²²Many will say to me on that day, 'Lord, Lord, did we not prophesy in your name and in your name drive out demons and in your name perform many miracles?' ²³Then I will tell them plainly, 'I never knew you. Away from me, you evildoers!'
> -Matthew 7:21-23 (NIV)

While it's true that God is gracious and delights in showing mercy to those who seek it, it's also true that some people are self-deceived regarding what it takes to receive that mercy. But who are the ones who are self-deceived? And who are those who will be declared righteous in God's sight? Well, before I address how a person can know he/she is right with God, we should first examine a deceptive cultural belief about God that is leading many astray. It's called Universalism, sometimes called Unitarianism. It's the belief that all spiritual paths lead to the same place, and that Jehovah, the God of the Bible, Who says He is the *only* God, can be reached pretty much any old way a person might choose or invent for himself. Let's briefly examine this in the light of common sense.

Believe it or not, there are some people who still claim that the earth is flat. If you have trouble believing that, just google "Flat Earth Society." It's true. They are out there. They walk among us. And they are sincere. But does the strength of their belief and the depth of their sincerity make their belief true? Two people cannot disagree on something and *both* be right! Someone is wrong!

What about spiritual matters, then? Can two people believe totally different things and both of them be correct just because they are both sincere? If all paths lead to God, where does that put pagan belief systems that embrace horrific acts like human sacrifice? Were ancient religions like those of the Canaanites one of the many ways to God? The Canaanites and other nations neighboring ancient Israel worshipped a god of their own making that they named, Molech. History records that the worship of Molech involved ritual child sacrifice by burning live babies to death. The Canaanites were sincere in their worship of Molech, apparently. And so are the modern-day witch doctors who practice human sacrifice in Uganda and other places throughout the world. But does that sincerity make them right with God?

For the record, by the way, the true God of Heaven made His feelings about this sort of evil perversion quite clear:

> **"Any one of the people of Israel or of the strangers who sojourn in Israel who gives any of his children to Molech shall surely be put to death. I myself will set My face against that man and will cut him off from among his people, because he has given one of his children to Molech, to make My sanctuary unclean and to profane My holy Name."**
> **-Leviticus 20:2-3** (ESV)

Clearly, the worship of Molech is not a way to be on good terms with God. What about other religions and belief systems, then? How about atheism, or Nazism? Are these legitimate ways to God? How about the belief systems of radical Muslim groups like ISIS which pride themselves in the murder of "infidels" who do not worship "Allah," and who torture and execute Christians and Jews in ways that are unimaginable? Is God pleased with them, too?

I could go on and on, but I hope you get the point. While it sounds like a very nice sentiment to suggest that people just need to be open-minded and that everyone is ultimately on their way to the same place regardless of what they believe, the fact is that that belief system is naïve to say the least. Think about it. To suggest that everyone is on good terms with God as long as they are "good" and "sincere" misses the mark of common sense by a mile. After all, the Canaanites were sincere, and the Nazis thought they were doing mankind a favor by murdering 6 million Jews and attempting to cleanse the human gene pool of their "flawed" DNA (a belief system that was heavily influenced in Darwinian evolution, by the way).

Here's where it gets dicey. Most people would agree that God would in no way condone what Hitler and the Nazis did, nor would He condone ritual child sacrifice. Yet we can't have it both ways. Either each and every path leads to God like Universalism suggests, or there are paths that don't, thus refuting Universalism. Clearly, if God exists and He is good, there are certain belief systems that He abhors. Hence, all paths do *not* lead to God!

So then, how do we know which paths *do* lead to God? Are they the ones that promote kindness instead of hate; good deeds instead of murdering one's enemies? The popular cultural belief seems to be something like this: "As long as I'm a good person who doesn't hurt anyone, I'll make it to heaven someday if there is one." Really? *That's* how people are planning their trip to eternity? It's okay, then, for a person to live by his or her own rules as long as those rules seem okay to him or her, just as long as those rules are dressed up by going to religious gatherings once in a while, wearing the label of Jew, Hindu, Muslim, or "Christian"? Will a label get you into heaven?

I put the word *Christian* in quotation marks here because statistics show that 83% of Americans identify themselves as Christians, according to abc.go.com and other research sources. Yet, Barna Research Group – a research group devoted to religious trends – shows that only about 7% of Americans hold to beliefs and practices that are consistent with the Christian faith as taught by the Bible. This is a modern-day example of the scenario quoted earlier from Matthew 7 where many people would approach Jesus on the Day of Judgment expecting mercy but who receive damnation instead. This is also a good explanation for why some people mistakenly believe they have been wronged or cheated by Christians. In reality, they were likely not cheated by a Christian at all, but by someone who falls in the category of that 83% of Americans who wear that label to appease their own consciences, but who nevertheless have no interest in actually being a disciple of Jesus.

On a side note, to anyone reading this who has been repelled by the Christian faith because of negative experiences with people who claim to be Christian, let me assure you that God knows those who are truly His. There are pretenders (hypocrites), and there are the true sheep. It is unfortunately the pretenders, the frauds, and the wolves in sheep's clothing who give the true sheep a bad name, the same way a few dishonest car salesmen give the entire profession a bad name. Jesus taught, however, that God the Father would separate the sheep from the goats and the wheat from the chaff on the Great Day of Judgment. It is also true that even true disciples of Jesus are still flawed people who are in process and who make mistakes and who sometimes inadvertently offend people. I myself have even said to God once or twice during times of frustration with church people, "I love You, Lord, but I don't like Your people very much." This is actually a statement of incredible pride, similar to how Jesus once described some people who think they can clearly see the speck of dust in their neighbor's eye but completely miss the log in their own.

While I would like to be able to say that all Christians perfectly represent the love and virtue of Jesus all the time, the fact is, that's not true, because we are all imperfect and learning to become more Christ-like throughout the courses of our lives. And that's the beauty of Christianity. When we come to God simply through faith in Jesus as our scapegoat and not by some impossible list of do's and don'ts, God forgives us and accepts us just like we are, flaws and all, and then He begins the process of character transformation slowly but surely, through trial and error, and through many mistakes and failures. Yes, there are a lot of Christians still in process, and there are also pretenders who are not what they seem. The wise person, however, will realize that all of mankind is in the same dire straits of being twisted by a sin nature. The difference between the true Christian and the non-Christian is that the Christian realizes his/her sinful state and seeks forgiveness, restoration, and rehabilitation through the transformative work of God through Jesus, whereas the non-Christian believes he/she can work it out on his/her own and somehow do enough good deeds to outweigh the bad.

Getting back to the point at hand, though, how then can a person know that the Christian faith is the way that God has planned for mankind to be right with Him?

Who is the God of the Bible, and What is He Like?

Most people attribute to God the qualities of love, mercy, and forgiveness. All these attributes are absolutely accurate. But God is not unjust or unmerciful to plan only one way to salvation. He is God, after all. He is perfectly reasonable to provide as many or as few ways to salvation as He likes. The Bible teaches that He has made only one way to be reconciled to Him.

> *"Jesus is 'the stone you builders rejected, which has become the cornerstone.' Salvation is found in no one else, for there is no other name under heaven given to mankind by which we must be saved."*
> **-Acts 4:11-12** (NIV)

This claim alone would invalidate Christianity as one of the many ways to God if, in fact, this claim is not true. How could God condone any religious system that makes false claims about Him? Hence, either this claim is absolutely true, or Christianity is a total fraud. There's no in-between.

Why Does Mankind Need to be Reconciled at All?

Before we examine the previous point further, let's first discuss why mankind needs to be reconciled to God at all. Doesn't God already love everyone, and isn't He already a God of mercy Who knows we are all prone to sins and mistakes, and Who will therefore overlook our sins?

The Bible is unique compared to all other religions of the world because unlike other religious systems that suggest that mankind is inherently good, or that we are able to offer good deeds and sacrifices to cleanse away sins and imperfections, the Bible teaches that mankind is born with a sin nature that is bent on pleasing itself and rebelling against God, and no amount of good deeds can bridge the gap between mankind's sin and God's perfect holiness. The inherent sin nature can be clearly demonstrated in how a parent doesn't have to teach a child how to lie, to throw temper tantrums, and to be totally selfish. These things come very naturally to fallen mankind and, therefore, do not need to be taught. Selfishness and sin is already in our DNA. What parents *do* have to teach children is how and why to share, to be honest, to exercise self-control, etc. These attributes do not come naturally to us.

Sin is defined as rebellion against God. Sin is knowing the standard but choosing to violate it. It can be compared to breaking the law. A person who knows it is wrong to steal but robs someone at gunpoint is a thief and an outlaw, even if he does it only once. God's system of law works exactly the same way. In fact, our system of law in the United States was established by our Founders based largely upon the Levitical Law found in the Old Testament of the Bible.

This is relevant to our discussion because a person cannot understand how God's judicial system works until one also understands how our earthly legal system works, because they are similar.

Let's say by way of example that you had a lapse in judgment one day and in an act of financial desperation decided to rob a convenience store and hold a clerk at gunpoint. Let's imagine things got out of control and you fired upon the attendant and killed him, and then ran off with the money. As you later stand convicted before a judge and he asks you what you have to say for yourself, in your defense you look for something to say – anything – that might cool the judge's wrath. So you mutter something foolish like this: "Judge, this is the first time I've ever done anything like this. I have had a totally clean record up until now. This was a momentary lapse in judgment because of a desperate financial situation. So because I'm basically a good person who just made a mistake, I would like to say that I believe you are also a good man, and I think you'll see that I deserve to be let me off easy."

Let's now turn our attention to the judge in this fictitious scenario. The judge might smirk a little before he answers. He might even laugh at you. He would most certainly shake his head in disbelief at your stupidity. And then he utters the words that you were hoping you would not have to hear: "Well, you're right about one thing; I AM a good man. And it's *because* I'm a good man who cares about justice that I'm going to see to it that justice is done and that you are punished for your crimes. You are a thief and a murderer, and I sentence you to life in prison."

What does this have to do with God's eternal justice? Everything! You see, God is a good God Who loves justice. Just like a judge would be an unjust and crooked judge to let a murderer go free just because it was his first offense, God likewise would be a perverter of justice if He let liars, thieves, adulterers, fornicators, blasphemers, and God-haters go free.

"But Andy, none of these things describe me. I'm a good person. I've made a few mistakes, but I think God and me are okay."

Well, in the spirit of making good plans for the most important trip you will ever take, let's examine that claim against what the Bible says. If you will stick with me a while longer, I'm leading up to some good news.

Who is Good in God's Sight?

Have you ever told a lie? What does that make you? Most people might object to the notion that telling a few lies makes a person a liar. But contemplate this question: How many people would you have to murder before being considered a murderer? One, right? By those same standards, and according to God's judicial system, if you tell one lie you are a liar. If you steal one thing that doesn't belong to you, you are a thief. If you use God's Holy Name as a swear word, you are a blasphemer. Jesus even taught that if you hate someone in your heart and curse them, you are guilty of murder in your heart. He also taught that a man who lusts in his heart and covets a woman not his wife is an adulterer. By the standard of God's perfect and Holy Law, He is judging mankind not just by the outward actions, but also by the secret thoughts and motives of the heart. And He doesn't grade on a curve. In other words, He doesn't judge you by how other people act and compare you to them. He judges you by *your* actions compared to His Holy Law.

So by those standards, when you stand before God on Judgment Day, will you be innocent or guilty? If you are honest, you would have to admit that you are a lying, thieving, adulterous, murderous, blasphemer, and you have no alibi.

This is why the Bible teaches that the Old Testament Law, which the Ten Commandments is a part, is not designed to save us, but to show us how much we need to be saved. The Law is designed to expose our inner corruptions and to stop the mouth of justification that claims, "I'm a good person." The Law is designed to drive us to our knees seeking forgiveness.

This is why the book of Romans says,

> *Obviously, the law applies to those to whom it was given, for its purpose is to keep people from having excuses, and to show that the entire world is guilty before God. For no one can ever be made*

right with God by doing what the law commands.
The law simply shows us how sinful we are.
-Romans 3:19-20 (NLT)

People who try to rely on their own conduct that is "good" in their own eyes will one day discover to their horror that they are under the judgment of God for the evils they have done both outwardly and inwardly. This includes some regular churchgoers who are relying on their church attendance to appease God's judgment against sin. Again, if God is truly good, then that goodness demands that He uphold justice and punish blasphemers, liars, thieves, fornicators, adulterers, etc., wherever they are found. What people hope will save them on the Day of Judgment, which is the goodness of God, is actually the very thing that will condemn them.

Now the Good News

The word, "gospel," means good news. The Gospel of Jesus Christ is good news, because now, through Jesus, guilty sinners don't have to be condemned as such. We can be declared "not guilty." How?

The Great Judge of the World provided a stand-in; a scapegoat; someone who paid your bail and took your punishment for you. God the Father sent a manifestation of Himself – Jesus, the Christ – Who came to earth for the ultimate purpose of taking upon Himself God's wrath against sin so that all who place their faith in Him would be cleansed of their sins, totally forgiven, and declared not guilty! When the perfect Son of God, Jesus, hung on the cross in agony, He took upon Himself what you and I deserved for our endless sins and rebellions against God. When we place our faith in Him and turn our lives over to Him, He takes what we have, which is our sin and guilt, and replaces it with His righteousness!

Pay very close attention to the following passage out of the book of Romans:

²¹But now God has shown us a way to be made right with him without keeping the requirements of the law, as was promised in the writings of Moses and the prophets long ago. ²²We are made right with God by placing our faith in Jesus Christ. And this is true for everyone who believes, no matter who we are. ²³For everyone has sinned; we all fall short of God's glorious standard. ²⁴Yet God, with undeserved kindness, declares that we are righteous. He did this through Christ Jesus when he freed us from the penalty for our sins. ²⁵For God presented Jesus as the sacrifice for sin. People are made right with God when they believe that Jesus sacrificed his life, shedding his blood. This sacrifice shows that God was being fair when he held back and did not punish those who sinned in times past, or he was looking ahead and including them in what he would do in this present time. God did this to demonstrate his righteousness, ²⁶for he himself is fair and just, and he declares sinners to be right in his sight when they believe in Jesus. ²⁷Can we boast, then, that we have done anything to be accepted by God? No, because our acquittal is not based on obeying the law. It is based on faith. ²⁸So we are made right with God through faith and not by obeying the law.

-Romans 3:21-28 (NLT)

But How Do We Know the Bible is True?

The answer to the question is a much bigger topic than I can adequately address in this short section to close out this book. I will offer some insights here, but I also encourage getting your hands on some of the wonderful and well-researched resources available that demonstrate the divinely-inspired nature of the Bible, such as those by former atheists Lee Strobel, Josh McDowell, and J. Warner Wallace, to name just a few. For non-readers, perhaps the

2017 movie, *The Case for Christ*, based on Lee Strobel's personal story of accepting Jesus as his savior after investigating the claims and resurrection of Jesus, could be a help here.

Many learned researchers over the years, including all three of the aforementioned authors, had set out to disprove the validity of the Holy Bible as divinely inspired, but have emerged from those endeavors as converted believers. Others worthy of mention are:

- Simon Greenleaf: one of the principle founders of Harvard Law School who was determined to use his genius-level skills in the principles of investigation to disprove the resurrection of Jesus Christ. Greenleaf wrote the book that all law students are required to study on the laws of evidence, and it was said of him that he knew more about the laws of evidence than all the lawyers who adorned the courts of Europe. After his exhaustive investigation into the claims of the Bible that Jesus Christ was raised from the dead, he renounced his atheism, became a devoted Christian, and spent the rest of his life as an ardent apologist for the Christian faith. He once wrote, "I can prove to any court in the land that Jesus Christ is an actual historical figure who lived and who was crucified according to Scripture, and who was raised from the dead three days after His execution."

- Sir William Ramsay, a 19th-Century archeologist, set out to disprove the writings of Luke the physician who wrote the account of the first Century Church in the Biblical book of Acts. Ramsay dedicated 25 years of his career to this pursuit, only to concede defeat and claim that Luke was one of the most accurate historians who ever lived!

- Sir Lionel Luckoo, an Indian-born British defense attorney of the early 20th Century, once set out to overturn the claim that Jesus rose from the dead. Luckoo was a brilliant investigator, so much so that he still holds the Guinness

World record for successfully defending an unprecedented 245 murder cases. Luckoo was an atheist, and he, too, set out to apply his deductive genius to overturning the Bible. But at the end of his exhaustive investigation, he came back believing in Jesus as God's son and the only way to salvation. He became a devoted Christian and an ardent defender of the faith and the Bible until his dying day. He once wrote, "The evidence for the resurrection of Jesus Christ is so overwhelming that it compels acceptance by proof that leaves absolutely no room for doubt."

- In more recent times, author and speaker, Josh McDowell, was an atheist in college and was challenged by a group of Christian students to investigate the claims of Jesus. He accepted that challenge with the confidence that he would prove wrong a group of people that he saw as intellectually beneath him. He too, however, came back believing, and Josh McDowell is still busy at work today defending the faith, having spoken to millions of college students during the span of his ministry. He has written the highly acclaimed books, *More than a Carpenter*, and, *Evidence that Demands a Verdict*, among several others.

Here are some brief insights on why we can count on the Bible as being truly inspired by God and Jesus as being the only way of salvation.

Fulfilled Prophecies

The fastest way for any religious belief system to discredit itself is by making predictions about the future, especially if those predictions do not come true. Yet the Bible is full of prophecies about the future, most of which have already been fulfilled in uncanny detail, including Isaiah's remarkable and detailed prediction about the Savior's crucifixion some 700 years before the Romans began using such torture. There are too many others to list here, so let's narrow our focus on a prophecy that defies explanation: The resurrection of Jesus Christ from the dead.

During Jesus' life on earth He predicted on numerous occasions that He would be crucified and then raised to life on the third day following His burial. One such prophecy is recorded in Matthew 20:17-19:

> ¹⁷*Now Jesus was going up to Jerusalem. On the way, he took the Twelve aside and said to them,* ¹⁸*"We are going up to Jerusalem, and the Son of Man will be delivered over to the chief priests and the teachers of the law. They will condemn him to death* ¹⁹*and will hand him over to the Gentiles to be mocked and flogged and crucified. On the third day he will be raised to life!"* (NIV)

If His predictions proved false, Jesus' followers would have been scattered and the Christian faith would have instantly died. Yet this has been the very point on which the researchers skeptical of the claims of Christianity have been snagged. As stated already, time after time skeptics and investigators have set out to disprove this historical event, yet many have come back believing that Jesus did indeed rise from the dead, and reliable historical records of the day support the fact that His disciples were still alive and in the general vicinity at the time and clearly would have been fully aware if the resurrection had been a hoax.

Entire books have been written on the mounds of evidence validating the resurrection account, more than I can even begin to record here. For the reader who wishes to investigate that evidence, any one of the previously-mentioned authors would be recommended for a thorough treatment of this subject.

One piece of evidence I will share here, though, pertains to the disciples of Jesus. History records that all but one of Jesus' disciples were put to gruesome and torturous deaths for their testimony about Jesus. They were willing to subject themselves to barbaric executions rather than to recant. As just stated, if the resurrection of Jesus were a hoax, they were in the position to know it. And no one is willing to be put to long and agonizing deaths for something they know to be a lie. When faced with recanting or else be sawn in two, a liar would quickly choose the former. While, perhaps, there may be an insane person who might choose death rather than to recant on a lie, the chances of ten men all choosing death over recanting is beyond the realm of possibility. They were all convinced by their own personal experience that Jesus had been raised from the dead and then ascended into heaven before their eyes.

This is obviously significant for many reasons. As stated already, if Jesus had not been raised from the dead as He predicted, then the Christian faith is altogether false and would have died in the first century. Yet Jesus *did* rise from the dead, thus validating His prophecies and His claims of being the only way to salvation.

The resurrection of Jesus is also significant for the simple fact that raising from the dead is impossible by human standards. The resurrection of a cold, dead, mutilated body is something only God could do. No other religious figure in history ever predicted his own death and resurrection, much less later validate those claims by actually doing it. Buddha is still dead in the ground today. So it Mohammed. Likewise with every other religious leader down through history. Jesus is the only one to ever break the power of death and rise to life, appearing to over 500 people over a period of about 40 days.

The Evidence Demands a Response

If the Bible is truly inspired by God, and if Jesus validated His claims of deity and of being the only way to salvation by rising from the dead as He predicted He would, then a response is demanded. The God of the Universe Who broke through time and space to enter the earth realm through the God-man, Jesus Christ, didn't go to the cross and die a criminal's death to pay the penalty for our sins just so we could make a few improvements on our behavior. He paid that penalty so that we humans who have been contaminated with sin and alienated from God and destined for eternal punishment could be declared "not guilty" and reconciled back to God and deemed the righteousness of God.

> [17]*This means that anyone who belongs to Christ has become a new person. The old life is gone; a new life has begun!* [18]*And all of this is a gift from God, who brought us back to himself through Christ. And God has given us this task of reconciling people to him.* [19]*For God was in Christ, reconciling the world to himself, no longer counting people's sins against them. And he gave us this wonderful message of reconciliation.* [20]*So we are Christ's ambassadors; God is making his appeal through us. We speak for Christ when we plead, "Come back to God!"* [21]*For God made Christ, who never sinned, to be the offering for our sin so that we could be made right with God through Christ.*
> *-2 Corinthians 5:17-21* (NLT)

So those who place their faith in Jesus as their scapegoat and follow Him as their Lord and Savior will be forgiven of their sins and declared the righteousness of God! And this is the first and most important step at being good at life, because planning for your eternal destiny is the most important planning you will ever do. The benefits to placing one's faith in God through Jesus Christ are not just for the afterlife, but also for here and now.

> *While bodily training is of some value, godliness is of value in every way, as it holds promise for the present life and also for the life to come.*
> *-1 Timothy 4:8* (ESV)

Last Thought: Count the Cost

This bonus chapter would be incomplete without mentioning the importance of counting the cost of following Christ, if, in fact, you are not already following Him. Being a follower of Christ means that you will make Him the LORD of your life, which means your supreme authority. No longer will you pursue you own self-serving agenda, but you will seek to please God in all your ways and follow God's design for your life. This is not bad news, but good news, because the God Who knows you better than yourself knows what is best for you, and He will direct your life toward significance, fulfilment, and peace, and becoming His manifestation of sacrificial love to others.

Along the way, however, there will be hurdles to overcome. Overcoming one's own sinful and selfish tendencies in order to pursue the character of Christ is not always easy. That road is fraught with personal failures and frustrations as you learn to say *no* to your selfish ways and *yes* to God. Along that road you will also likely experience the reality of persecution for righteousness sake. You may lose friendships over your commitment to follow Christ and your seeking to be transformed into His image. In fact, it's almost certain you will. You may even lose relationships with family members. Jesus said that this would be a strong possibility (see Matthew 10:34-36). If you choose to allow your life to be truly directed by the Holy Spirit and the guidance of God's Word in a way that is beyond compromise, you will likely stand out among even many churchgoers who are simply "cultural Christians," – those who are Christians in name only but not really in practice. Just as it was in Jesus' time, you may be labeled as a fanatic and an extremist by even many religious people. Yet what we give up for the Kingdom of God is far outweighed by the rewards of following Him; in this life, yes, but even more so in our heavenly home.

If you have not already made Jesus your Lord and Savior, that commitment is no harder than simply crying out to God in repentance and seeking His forgiveness, and then placing your faith in Him as your stand-in – the scapegoat for your sins – and setting your heart to following Him for the rest of your days. It's not important to get hung up on the words you pray, because God is looking for the cry of your heart. Yet, because I know that some people can be at a loss for words in addressing the God of the Universe, allow me give you a template prayer that you might follow. Pray something like this:

"Lord God of heaven, I know I don't deserve to even draw my next breath, let alone speak to you. I am a sinful person; I know that. I have sinned against you all my life, and I have no excuses. I acknowledge that because of my self-centered ways and my rebellion against your commands, I deserve your judgment. But I come to you in faith, acknowledging that Jesus took my punishment for me on the cross and died for my sins. I believe what your Word says in 2 Corinthians 5:21 that even though Jesus had no sin, He became sin for me on the cross so that I might be declared the righteousness of God. So Father God, I throw myself upon your mercy and your love, and here and now I place my faith in Jesus Christ as my Savior and Lord, asking you to forgive my many sins and make me your righteousness. As of this moment, I promise to follow You, Lord, and I turn my life over to you to remake me into the image of Christ according to Your good pleasure. Fill me with Your Holy Spirit right now, and empower me with your strength to live for You."

If you prayed this prayer, I encourage you to follow through and find a good, uncompromising, Bible-believing church where you can get baptized as Jesus commanded, where you can get involved with other Christians who will love and support you, and where you can receive good instruction and teaching.

Unfortunately, it is more difficult than ever to find churches that are preaching and teaching the full, uncompromised message of the Gospel, because we are living in the time predicted in the Scriptures where it says that the day will come when there will be people who have "a form of godliness but who deny its power" (see 2 Timothy 3:1-7). Even so, the Spirit of God can direct you. Pray and ask Him to help you find a church that is a solid, uncompromising fellowship where you can grow in your faith.

If wish to know more, feel free to contact me at my ministry website, at AndrewRobbinsMinistries.org.

I leave you with the prayer of the Apostle Paul when he wrote to the Corinthian Christians. This is my prayer for you as you sojourn through this life.

> [16]*I pray that out of his glorious riches he may strengthen you with power through his Spirit in your inner being, [17]so that Christ may dwell in your hearts through faith. And I pray that you, being rooted and established in love, [18]may have power, together with all the Lord's holy people, to grasp how wide and long and high and deep is the love of Christ, [19]and to know this love that surpasses knowledge—that you may be filled to the measure of all the fullness of God.*
> **-Ephesians 3:16-19** (NIV)

Bibliography

1. Tony Cooke, *Qualified: Serving God with Integrity and Finishing Your Course with Honor*, Harrison House Publishers, 2012; chapter 10, *Intentional Integrity*
2. Nightingale Conant, *The Top 2%: What it Takes to Reach the Top in Your Profession*, Simple Truths, LLC, 2012
3. Ray Comfort, *Hell's Best Kept Secret (audio)*, LivingWaters.com
4. Steven K. Scott, *The Richest Man Who Ever Lived: King Solomon's Secrets to Success, Wealth, and Happiness*, Kindle Edition, 2006, Crown Business
5. Craig Brian Larson and Leadership Journal, *750 Engaging Illustrations for Preachers, Teachers, and Writers*, Baker Books, 2004
6. Brian Cavanaugh, *Don't Rest on Laurels (article)*, Leadership By Design, March 2011, Volume 3, Issue 3, archive.constantcontact.com

About the Author

Andrew G. Robbins is the founder of Andrew Robbins Ministries (A.R.M), and he and his wife, Donna, are the founders of Blessed Life Fellowship in south/central Indiana where he has pastored since 2010. His other books and ministry materials can be found at AndrewRobbinsMinistries.org, and BlessedLifeFellowship.org.

Printed in the United States
By Bookmasters